Stephen Russ

practical screen printing

Studio Vista London
Watson-Guptill Publications New York

Acknowledgements

I am grateful to all the artists and printers whose work has been used to illustrate this book, and to the owners who have granted permission for their prints to be reproduced. For the prints by children and students I am indebted to Bishop Bright Grammar School, Leamington Spa; Dartington College of Arts; Fitzmaurice Grammar School, Bradford-on-Avon; Newton Park College of Education, Bath.

I would like to acknowledge with thanks the help I have had from the British Museum, the Horniman Museum, the Victoria and Albert Museum, and the Printing Library, St Bride Foundation Institute, London; the Pitt Rivers Museum, Oxford; the City Museum, Bristol; the American Museum in Britain, Claverton; the City of Bath Reference Library; and the Museum of Modern Art, New York.

For advice on technical matters I have appealed in every case to the specialist manufacturers, and I am grateful to them for their help, and for allowing me to make use of their literature. For settling any questions of chemistry, I have always turned to my friend Mr Clive Eastman.

The quotations from *Il libro dell'Arte* are taken from Christine Herringham's translation, *The Book of the Art of Cennino Cennini*. They are reproduced by the courtesy of the publisher, George Allen and Unwin Ltd.

The following illustrations are reproduced by kind permission of: The Swiss Silk Bolting Cloth Mfg Co, Gallen, St Thal, Switzerland (plate 3); Selectarine Silk Screens Ltd, London (plate 15); D. Gottlieb & Co., Chicago (plate 19).

Finally, may I thank the photographers who have taken the plates specially for this book, Miss Gene Cox of South West Optical Instruments, Mr Richard Morling and Mr Euan Wannop.

© Stephen Russ 1969
Published in Great Britain by Studio Vista Limited
Blue Star House, Highgate Hill, London N19
and in New York by Watson-Guptill Publications
165 West 46th Street, New York, New York 10036
Library of Congress Catalog Card Number 70-82272
Set in Plantin 110 11 on 13 pt
Printed in Great Britain by
Staples Printers Limited

SBN 289 27852 X

Contents

Introduction

Nobody knows who invented the screen process, or when or where the invention took place. A definitive history of the craft has yet to make its appearance.

There can be no doubt that the screen has evolved from the ordinary stencil, where colour is forced through holes cut in a thin flat sheet. Ordinary stencilling is known all over the world; it is practised by Eskimos and by Fiji Islanders. The earliest examples are found among Palaeolithic cave paintings dating from 30,000 BC. But if we were looking for the place where the screen might have been invented, it would be natural to go to Japan, for the Japanese are the most expert stencil cutters in the world.

In the years between 1639 and 1854, Japan sealed herself off from almost all contact with the outside world, but during this period some examples of Japanese manufacture found their way to Europe in the holds of Dutch ships trading out of Nagasaki. Some of these examples had been decorated by a strange type of printing: it looked like stencilling, and yet it could not possibly have been done by an ordinary stencil. The elements were widely scattered, and in place of the usual thick white bars or ties there appeared the faint shadow of a network of hair-like threads. These prints had been stencilled through a screen. An examination of the few, very rare and fragile surviving screens, shows that the threads did indeed consist of single strands of human hair, stretched tight and glued to a rectangular frame. The stencil itself was often cut in duplicate, with the two copies glued face to face, gripping the net between them.

The next time we hear of the screen is in North America where, in the years around 1900, it was being used by display men and signwriters to speed up production of their repetition jobs. It is difficult to imagine what kind of connection there might have been between the Japanese hair stencil and the first American screen. No evidence has yet been brought forward to prove beyond doubt that there was a connection. It may well be that the American version presented itself to its unknown inventor spontaneously and independently.

The first American screens were covered with cotton organdie. In the very early days the cotton was used simply as a support for a cut paper stencil, but it was not long before somebody discovered that liquid fillers could be applied direct to the mesh itself. From that moment on, the craft has never looked back.

Fig. 1 Stencilled decoration in starch resist, Yoruba, mid-twentieth century

1 The screen frame

If we visit any screen printing workshop, we are sure to see, running along one wall, a library of screen frames stored like books on shelves. The frames will be all of a standard size and the shelves will be built to fit them. Perhaps there will be two standard sizes or even three but if it is a well-planned workshop we are not likely to find a rabble of intermediate sizes. When setting up in screen printing for the first time, there is everything to be said for choosing the frame size with great care and then using it as a standard measure for all the other equipment.

The choice of frame size depends on the kind of work it is proposed to print. Nobody can tell in advance exactly what jobs will come along but most printers find that as their experience and confidence grow, so does their appetite for larger and larger prints.

A frame with internal dimensions of 24 in. × 38 in. will take prints up to 20 in. × 30 in. and this is a very popular size. A frame measuring 12 in. × 18 in. will take prints up to 9 in. × 12 in. and this is an excellent size for beginners. With such a frame it is possible, at very little cost, to do practical work in all branches of the craft.

A screen frame must be strong, reasonably light in weight, reasonably cheap to make and, above all, it must be accurately made so that it will lie flat on the printing bed.

Trade printers today are taking an increasing interest in metal frames and there is no reason why the amateur should not use them: they are available from the specialist suppliers. But most frames are made of wood. As so much in this craft depends on the frame, it is worth going to some trouble to look out some first quality clear, dry, straight-grained, knot-free softwood such as spruce, Douglas fir, or pine. Parana pine is not suitable because it warps so badly. Western red cedar is popular with textile printers because it is unaffected by water and also because it is light in weight. Textile printing screens are normally very large and they have to be lifted by hand after every print without benefit of hoist or counterbalance.

The larger the frame, the thicker the sides must be, thus:

SCREEN LENGTH	FRAME THICKNESS
Under 18 in.	1 in. square
18 in. to 24 in.	$1\frac{1}{4}$ in. square
24 in. to 36 in.	$1\frac{1}{2}$ in. square
36 in. to 48 in.	2 in. square

The cross section of the frame need not be a square. Indeed for large frames it would be better to use a section $1\frac{1}{2}$ in. × $2\frac{1}{2}$ in., assembled with the $2\frac{1}{2}$ in. face lying flat. This is stronger and lighter than a section 2 in. × 2 in.

The amateur woodworker could make his own frames or they could be built to order by any country joiner or carpenter. There are no special difficulties, and fancy corner joints are not called for. The joint known as the half-lap is good enough for any frame, provided it is accurately cut, glued with a strong waterproof glue ('Aerolite', 'Cascamite' or Elmer's glue) and screwed with brass screws.

Frames up to about 12 in. × 18 in. can be put together with simple butt-nailing at the corners. The difficulty with this kind of assembly is to end up with a frame that lies flat. The secret of success is:

1 Make all the saw cuts with perfect accuracy: they really must be 90°.

2 Before putting the frame together, set the nails in position at the ends of the side members. Drive them in until their points come through.

3 Arrange the parts of the frame flat on the bench and pressed hard up against the bench stop. Drive home the nails with horizontal blows, the head of the hammer lying on its side and skimming along the surface of the bench.

This is a quick method, and it can be used when a large frame has to be assembled in a hurry for a rush job.

When the glue has set, the frame must be tested to see that it lies flat. Hold it against a sheet of plate glass or marble or steel or any surface that is known to be absolutely flat. Lay the finger tips on the diagonally opposite corners of the frame and try to make it rock. This is a very exacting test; even the smallest error will be felt at once. If there is any error, this must be corrected by planing.

Lastly, round off all the outside edges and corners by sandpapering. Leave all the inside edges square. Coat the finished frame with two or three applications of polyurethane varnish or orange shellac. This will seal the pores of the wood, keep the frame dry and reduce the danger of warping.

2 The mesh

The silk screen process gets its name from the finely woven silk gauze or mesh stretched across the frame. From the very beginning silk has proved itself to be the almost perfect mesh material, and even now old-fashioned printers are inclined, from force of habit, to call everything in a frame silk. But silk is by no means the only fabric used in screens. At one time or another practically every other likely material has been tried. Linen, wool and rayon have been found unsuitable. Cotton organdie is still in regular use wherever low cost is the first consideration. Phosphor-bronze and stainless steel are sometimes used in industry. And ever since 1938, when nylon was first introduced to the world, the position of all these materials has been challenged by the man-made fibres.

In effect, the screen printer's mesh is a sieve; the space between the threads is as important as the threads themselves. The weave must be open; that is to say there must be enough threads to support the stencil, but not so many as to obstruct the free passage of the printing colour. The individual threads must be thin and smooth, strong and reasonably elastic. A good screen should be as tight as a drum and, ideally, it should remain so at all times. Even if we soak it in water, or store it for weeks in a drying rack, or heat it under an electric iron, we would like our mesh to stay tight. What we are looking for is a fabric with a self-adjusting tension. How near any mesh comes up to this ideal, or falls below it, depends more than anything else on the physical properties of the fibre from which it is woven.

Cotton

Under the microscope a single fibre of cotton looks like a flattened tube, twisted and shrivelled. The thread spun up from it has an irregular, crumpled surface. These irregularities provide a good grip or key to any kind of gum, glue, starch, varnish, lacquer or paint. All types of stencil will adhere well to cotton. On the other hand, a surface like this tends to accumulate deposits of printing colour and if care is not taken, the mesh may become choked. If printing is interrupted even for a short time, the screen may set solid.

The cotton thread has a moderate tensile strength but poor elasticity. It shrinks when wet and becomes slack again as it dries out. This alternation can lead to distorted images and difficulty in registration.

The cotton organdie specially made for screen printing has a simple square weave with a count of about 90 threads to the lineal inch. As a substitute, good dressmakers' organdie can be used and for very simple styles of work and short runs it is even possible to print with butter muslin or cheese cloth.

Cotton is by far the cheapest mesh material – silk costs five times as much. It is the obvious choice for short rush jobs where a more expensive fabric would not be justified. And it is the ideal material for beginners.

Silk

The silk used by screen printers comes from the cocoon spun by the cultivated silkworm, the caterpillar of the moth *Bombyx mori*. The silk is generated as a liquid in two glands in the silkworm's head and emerges as a double filament bonded and coated with a natural gum called sericin. Spinning continues for two or three days and by the end of this time the silkworm will have produced anything up to a mile of silk, all in one continuous strand.

A strand of raw silk is straw coloured and stiff, with microscopic creases and wrinkles in the sericin coating. These irregularities give a good grip to all types of stencil. Silk is a strong, resilient fibre. It tightens up when wet and relaxes slightly as it dries out but it never becomes really slack, as cotton does. It is hard wearing and, with careful treatment, will outlast ten cotton organdie screens.

The technique of weaving very fine silk gauze was well established in the western world long before the invention of screen printing. In the milling of wheat and other cereals, the grain is first crushed and then fed into a complex chain of sieving and grading operations collectively known as bolting. An essential part of the bolting apparatus is a nest of sieves through which the crushed particles are shaken and graded according to size. The sieves are covered with a fine silk gauze known as bolting cloth. This material has an ingenious woven structure: the weft threads run as a pair and as they pass between each warp thread and the next they are given a twist like a rope. Thus, although it is an open weave, the interlocked structure keeps it rigid, and the aperture size will remain constant even under stress. With remarkable perception, the early screen printers recognised that silk bolting cloth was exactly what they needed for their new craft.

Apart from bolting cloth, the silk weavers make another type of mesh known as taffeta. This has a plain square weave like cotton organdie. Taffeta can be woven finer and thinner than bolting cloth and for this reason it is preferred by screen printers using photographic techniques. It is less hard wearing but much cheaper than bolting cloth. The artist printer could hardly find a more attractive material.

Polyamide fibres (nylon)

In 1928 the American chemical manufacturers E. I. du Pont Nemours and Co. appointed an organic chemist from Harvard, Wallace H. Carothers, to lead a team of scientists in a programme of research into the properties of the long chain molecules. During the course of their work, the team produced and investigated a new substance which appeared to behave rather like silk: from a liquid state it could be drawn out into a long continuous filament. This substance was to become the first entirely man-made fibre. On 27 October 1938, it was introduced to the world as 'nylon'.

The nylon filament is as smooth as a glass rod. It is immensely strong, elastic, and resistant to abrasion. Even the thinnest meshes woven from the finest filaments are tough and hard wearing. The screen printer's mesh consists of single (monofilament) strands woven in a plain square weave. After weaving, the fabric is subjected to a heat treatment which fuses the warp and weft together at every intersection. In this way the aperture size is permanently set.

Nylon is a difficult fibre to stretch on the frame by hand, and some form of mechanical assistance is almost essential. Once it has been pulled tight nylon holds its tension very well: alternate wetting and drying produce very little distortion. It is unaffected by the chemicals and solvents normally used by the artist printer but it is affected by heat – it melts at 482°F (250°C). Great care must be taken when using a hot iron for fixing knife-cut stencils.

Polyester fibres (Terylene, Dacron)

The success of nylon was sufficient to galvanize chemical manufacturers all over the world and only three years elapsed before another major discovery was announced. In 1941, J. T. Dickson and J. R. Whinfield, working in the laboratory of the Calico Printers' Association in Lancashire, produced a new polymer which, like nylon, could be drawn out from a molten state into a long continuous filament. This was the synthetic polyester fibre. Large-scale production was delayed until after the war, when manufacturing rights were bought by Imperial Chemical Industries Ltd in the UK and by E. I. du Pont Nemours in the USA. The fibre is marketed by these two houses under the trade names 'Terylene' and 'Dacron' respectively.

The individual polyester fibre looks very like a fibre of nylon or spun glass. It is tough, resilient and unaffected by the chemicals and solvents normally used by the artist printer. It absorbs practically no water – ten times less than nylon – and fluctuations in tension are negligible. It softens at 230°C and melts at 260°C and so care must be taken when using a hot iron to stick knife-cut stencils.

Polyester fibre is manufactured in two forms, single strand (monofilament) and twisted yarn (multifilament) and both of these are used in the making of screen meshes. As would be expected, a monofilament mesh gives smooth printing and easy washing out but it also means there will be difficulty in getting some types of stencil to stick. The multifilament mesh is much less troublesome in this respect, because the surface of the twisted strand is naturally intricate and most stencils can be made to stick to it.

When stretching a polyester mesh on the frame some kind of mechanical stretcher is essential: this will be dealt with in the next chapter. But once it has been pulled tight a polyester mesh will stay tight. Here is what we have been looking for, a fabric with a self-adjusting tension.

A highly specialized branch of the textile industry, located chiefly in Switzerland, is devoted exclusively to the manufacture of these mesh materials. Both spinning and weaving are controlled with scrupulous accuracy down to exceedingly fine limits. The threads are spun in a standard range of thicknesses from fine to coarse, indicated by a set of conventional code letters, thus: S (light, for special purposes), M (light to medium), T (medium), HD (heavy duty). Silk bolting cloth alone continues to use the old silk code, thus: S (standard), X (medium), XX (heavy duty). Cotton organdie falls outside this system of classification.

All types of screen fabrics are measured by counting the mesh. A ruler is laid along one of the weft threads and the mesh count is the number of warp threads that cross it in an inch. The higher the mesh count, the smaller the apertures in the weave. Cotton organdie has a count of about 90 threads to the inch. Nylon can be had with a count of 460. This is far finer than the artist printer would ever use in practice. The ordinary working range is shown in the accompanying table. On the top line is the conventional code number by which the mesh is described, on the lower line is the mesh count in threads per inch.

CODE NUMBER	6	8	9	10	11	12	14	15	16	18	20
MESH COUNT	74	86	98	109	117	126	139	150	157	168	173

The code letter indicating the thickness of the thread is written after the code number describing the mesh. For example, silk bolting cloth 8 xx is woven from a heavy duty yarn and has a mesh count of 86 threads per inch. Such a mesh would be an excellent choice for all kinds of bold and open prints on textiles and on paper.

The finer the detail in the design and the finer the surface on which the print is to be made, the higher the mesh count must be. Photographic work involving fine lines and dots should have a mesh NO. 14 (139 threads per inch) or even finer.

A fine mesh will give a thin deposit of printing ink, a coarse mesh will give a thick deposit. Indeed the thickness of the ink deposit is directly governed by the thickness of the screen mesh. Certain types of inks, for instance the fluorescent colours and those containing metallic powders, must be given a coarse mesh or they will seize up.

A well-equipped screen printing workshop would carry in stock a wide range of meshes to cover every situation, but this is out of the question for the individual artist. What he needs is a happy compromise. Perhaps the best choice would be a NO. 10 (T), with a count of 109 threads to the inch.

All types of screen mesh are delicate and beautifully made fabrics and they deserve to be treated with care. When stretched on a frame they are easily punctured. A screen should never be dropped from a height, leant against a sharp object, or stood near a fire. But this kind of extreme rough handling is a rare occurrence. By far the commonest cause of damage is neglect; walking away at the end of the printing run, and leaving the ink to dry in the mesh. This should never be allowed to happen.

3 Stretching the mesh

Stretching the mesh on the frame, as with everything else in the silk screen process, can be done in a hundred and one different ways. The object is to stretch the fabric as tight as a drum, with the warp and weft threads correctly aligned with the sides of the frame, and then to fasten it in such a way that it will not come off.

The simplest method is by pinning, tacking, or stapling, just as a canvas is tacked to a stretcher. Cut the fabric with enough spare to grip and turn up on all four sides of the frame. Put in the first tack half way down one of the long sides, and then stretch the fabric across to the other long side and put in the second tack exactly opposite the first. Now stretch the material the other way and put in tacks 3 and 4 at the centre points of the two short ends of the frame. If this has been done properly there will now be a zone of tension in the shape of a cross, the line between tacks 1 and 2 being at right angles to the line between tacks 3 and 4. When stretching the fabric across the frame from one tack to its opposite number, the pull should always follow a thread. Now work methodically outwards an inch at a time from the first set of tacks, every tack put in on one side being immediately answered by a corresponding tack on the opposite side. In this way the cross-shaped zone of tension will spread wider and wider until it arrives at the corners of the frame.

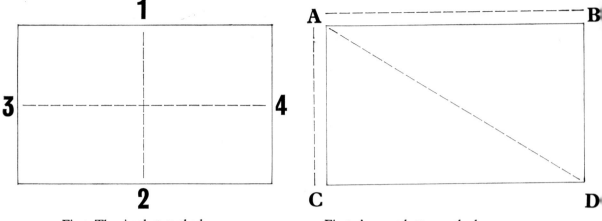

Fig 2 The simplest method   Fig 3 An even better method

An even better method is to begin at one corner, let us call it A, and work outwards from there, first down a long side and then down a short. Arrange the mesh material so that the selvedge lies along one of the long sides of the frame. Let us call this side AB. Put in a cluster of tacks at A, stretch the selvedge as tight as possible and put in a tack at B. Fasten down the side AB with tacks spaced about an inch apart, taking care not to distort the straight run of the selvedge. Now go back to corner A and stretch the fabric the other way, that is, along the short end of the frame to corner D, making sure that the weft threads are correctly aligned with the frame and at right angles to the selvedge. Put in a tack at D and then fasten down the whole of side AD with tacks spaced an inch apart. Next, go to corner C, the corner diagonally opposite to corner A, and pull the fabric as hard as possible along this diagonal. Put in a temporary tack at C. Have a close look at the warp and weft threads leading away from this tack. If all has gone well, it will be possible to trace them back to their starting points at B and D. Fasten down side DC with tacks spaced an inch apart, beginning at D. Fasten down side BC, beginning at B.

The tacking can be done with drawing pins, thumb tacks, blue tacks, or steel staples driven in by a gun tacker. Pins and tacks should not be driven all the way in, or it will be unnecessarily difficult to get them out later. If staples are driven in through a strip of card or linen tape, it will be easier to prise them out without damaging the frame. If an adhesive is to be used to supplement and reinforce the tacking, one line of tacks is strong enough, but if the tacks have to take the whole of the strain, they should be set in a double, staggered row. At the end of the job the tacks can be retrieved and used over and over again.

The adhesive used to fasten the mesh to the frame must be waterproof and strong. In recent years synthetic resin adhesives have been formulated for this particular purpose: they consist of a syrup and a catalyst which have to be mixed together immediately before use. The setting time is only about fifteen minutes, and the end product is absolutely waterproof and immensely strong. Examples of this type are Serifix made by Screen Process Supplies Ltd, and L.20 made in Germany by Albert Rose. Chemically quite different from these, Evo-Stik Impact Adhesive NO. 528 is an excellent alternative, and this is obtainable in all good tool shops in Great Britain. (In the US, Elmer's Glue is good.) A casein glue, such as Casco Grade A is also effective if given a protective coating of shellac or varnish when dry. Glues of the urea/formaldehyde type have been found to attack cotton. When you are using any of these modern glues, the makers' instructions must always be followed with scrupulous care.

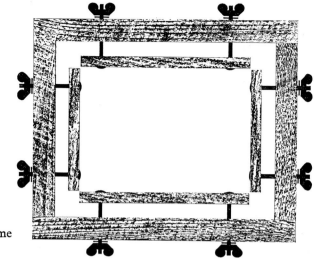

Fig 4 Master frame

It is not easy with the bare hands to pull a mesh drum tight. With a pair of canvas stretching pliers, or even a pair of ordinary pliers, the work is somewhat easier. But the easiest, quickest and best way to stretch any kind of mesh is to use a master frame.

This is a separate piece of equipment designed to fit outside the largest screen frame in the workshop. It consists of a strongly built rectangular outer frame and four separate inner pieces connected to the main frame by long bolts and wing nuts. These inner pieces are called floating bars and they can be pulled up tight to the outer frame or set at a distance in from it by adjusting the wing nuts. The apparatus is placed flat on a bench top and the screen frame to be covered is laid in the centre. The wing nuts are slacked off and the floating bars pushed inwards until they meet the sides of the screen frame. The mesh material is now stretched tight across the screen frame and pinned to the floating bars, taking care to align the warp and weft with the sides of the frame. By tightening up the wing nuts, the floating bars will be drawn outwards and the mesh pulled tight. When it is fully stretched a generous coating of adhesive is applied to the mesh where it lies in contact with the screen frame. Use a synthetic resin adhesive and spread it with a scrap of stiff card. As soon as the adhesive is set, the newly covered screen can be cut free by running a sharp knife along the gap between the screen frame and the floating bars. A master frame of this type can be used equally well to cover a number of smaller frames simultaneously. They can be packed in side by side, and cut apart at the end.

Another good method makes use of a simple tightening device on the screen frame itself. Tack a narrow strip of softwood – say 1 in $\times \frac{3}{8}$ in. – all round the face side of the frame so as to make a stepped or rebated profile. Round off the edges of the steps with sandpaper. Stretch the mesh as tight as possible by hand and tack and glue it to the outside of the frame, but not to the face side. Now take four more strips of 1 in. $\times \frac{3}{8}$ in. softwood, sand them smooth, and set in each a row of small panel pins (NO. 4 carpet tacks) spaced about three inches apart. With these strips, force the mesh down into the angle of the rebate. Fix everything in place by hammering home the panel pins. This primitive method will tighten even a nylon mesh; it will split a cotton one.

A method suitable for cotton takes advantage of the fact that paper expands when wet and shrinks as it dries out. Begin by stretching the mesh in the usual way, and tack to the outside edge of the frame but not to the face side. Make up a batch of casein glue in cold water according to the maker's instructions and apply it to the mesh all round the outside edge, in among the tacks. A cheap mop for applying this glue can be made by tying a strip of foam sheeting round the end of a stick. The active part of this method consists of four strips of newspaper glued to the face side of the screen as a border or mount. They should be cut about one inch wider than the wooden sides of the frame, so that when they are in position the extra inch will cover up part of the picture space. It is this overlap that does the work: the greater the overlap, the greater the pull when the glue dries. Give the strips a generous coating of casein glue, taking care not to get any on the back, and leave for about ten minutes for the glue to soak in. During this time the paper will expand by something like $\frac{1}{8}$ in. in every foot. Lay the strips carefully on the screen and smooth out with the finger tips. Now turn the screen over on to a clean place and rub the finger up and down the inside edges, pressing the mesh into the glued side of the newspaper strips. Add more glue if there is not enough. Turn the frame face up once more and leave to dry. As the glue dries, the paper will shrink and tighten the mesh. Retrieve the tacks and give all the glued surfaces a protective coating of shellac or, better still, polyurethane varnish.

4 Squeegees and scrapers

The tool used to press the colour through the screen is a squeegee. This consists of a straight-edged flexible blade backed by a stiff wooden holder. In action the squeegee traverses the inside of the screen from end to end, sweeping the colour before it. As it passes over the open parts of the stencil, the colour is forced through the mesh and the print is made.

Most squeegee blades are made of rubber. This comes in white or black; hard, medium or soft. White is better than black, as black rubber is inclined to tinge certain printing colours, notably lemon yellow. Squeegee blades are also made in synthetic plastics such as neoprene and polyurethane. Neoprene is black and hard and costs only slightly more than rubber. Polyurethane is the ideal material. It costs three times as much as rubber, but it has exactly the right degree of spring, it resists abrasion, it is easy to clean, and it is unaffected by the printer's chemicals and solvents. All these materials are manufactured in the form of running strip, cut to order and sold by the inch. The standard cross sections are 2 in. $\times$ $\frac{1}{4}$ in. and 2 in. $\times \frac{3}{8}$ in. For all squeegees over a foot long the thicker blade is recommended.

Fig 5 Cross section of squeegee

The blade is set in a wooden handle to keep it stiff and straight. A machine-made handle is channelled on the underside to take the blade, and the back is rounded so as to fit comfortably in the palm of the hand. A similar handle can be built up from three strips of wood glued together with waterproof glue. A very simple construction suitable for squeegees up to about 12 in. long consists of two side cheeks and a back glued direct to the rubber blade with an impact adhesive. The timber for this construction should be softwood strip with

Fig 6 A squeegee handle built up from three separate pieces of wood

a section 1 in. × ⅜ in. Allow the back strip to extend an inch beyond the blade at each end. During printing these projections will rest on the sides of the screen frame and prevent the squeegee from falling into the pool of colour. This little squeegee can be made at home in half an hour and will last for years.

The length of a squeegee is determined by the inside width of the screen frame: it should fit more or less right across from side to side, so that the whole surface of the silk is covered in one sweep. Between the ends of the squeegee and the sides of the frame there should be a small clearance but this need never be more than half an inch.

Handling a squeegee is almost the only purely physical skill that the beginner has to acquire. Take the handle in both hands, reach to the far end of the frame, drop the blade

Fig 7 Improvised squeegee

behind the pool of colour and pull towards you. The stroke must be smooth, unhesitating and firm. Considerable pressure is required. The blade must be kept sprung like a bow: if it is allowed to trail, additional pressure will only make matters worse. The whole effort should be concentrated in the leading edge of the blade. If things are going well, it should be possible to feel the texture of the silk in the palms of the hands. If the squeegee scrapes the inside of the screen clean, this is a good sign: if it leaves behind it a slick of colour, this is a bad sign.

The action of printing wears down the squeegee blade, and in time the bright new edge will become rounded. When this happens there will be a noticeable change in the quality of the prints. A rounded blade gives a thicker deposit of ink and less sharp definition of detail. Textile printers often prefer, when aiming at a saturated print, to work with a rounded squeegee blade. But if thin films of ink and fine detail are wanted, the blade must be kept sharp and the easiest way to do this is to grind the edge against a sheet of medium emery or garnet paper glued to a flat board. A guide rail at the side will help to keep the squeegee upright. Never attempt to trim a squeegee blade with a knife.

The squeegee is to the screen printer what the brush is to the painter, and it ought to be treated with care. Never drop it or leave it resting against a sharp object, never stand it near a fire or electric iron. And always make sure that the blade is perfectly clean before putting it away.

Sooner or later the printer will need to know how to coat a screen. This is a special art: it means applying to the mesh a thin even film of liquid filler. Coatings of this kind are an essential part of the so-called glue and tusche method, they are used in one style of photographic work and they can be used at any time as a quick and easy way of masking out unwanted areas in the mesh.

The filler can be applied with an ordinary squeegee but it is better to use a scraper kept for the purpose: a strip of metal or stiff plastic or, on a small scale, a scrap of cardboard.

Prepare the screen by waterproofing the mesh at the two narrow ends. This is to provide a floor on which the coating liquid can lie at the beginning and end of the stroke. The waterproofed zone should extend right across the mesh from side to side and it should not be less than three inches broad in small screens, proportionally more in large screens. In the jargon of the trade these zones are known as 'harbours', 'banks', or 'wells'. A permanent well can be made with lacquer or polyurethane varnish brushed into the mesh. A temporary well can be made with gummed paper strip, masking tape, or one of the self-adhesive protective foils, such as Fablon (trade name, UK).

Now prop up the screen on a couple of blocks of wood so that the mesh is lifted clear of the table. Pour a generous pool of the coating liquid into the well at one end, making sure that it is evenly distributed across the whole width. Insert the scraper between the end of the frame and the pool of coating liquid and incline the blade forward at an angle of about 60° as if it were a squeegee. Then, using moderate pressure, sweep the length of the screen in one steady stroke. That is all. Scrape up the surplus liquid and return it to the container. Leave the screen in a horizontal position until dry.

As far as possible, aim to keep the coating on the top surface of the mesh only; the less it gets through to the underside the better. It is easier to achieve this if the screen is held at a slope during the operation. The coating liquid is poured into the well at the bottom of the slope and then, with one firm steady stroke, swept uphill. At the end of the stroke the screen is immediately lowered to a horizontal position, propped clear of the table and left to dry.

The steeper the slope at which the screen is held, the less the coating liquid will tend to get through to the underside of the mesh. If it can be held in a vertical plane, so much the better: some craftsmen even go beyond this and hold the screen so that it is actually overhanging. If the screen can be fixed in an artists' easel, this leaves both hands free to hold the scraper.

But the best tool for applying all kinds of liquid filler is not a scraper but a coating trough. This consists of a length of metal or stiff plastic U or V channel closed at both ends. The edge of the trough acts as a scraper. The screen to be coated is set up vertically or slightly overhanging, and the trough, filled with coating liquid, is pressed against the mesh as low down as possible. By tilting the trough gently, the liquid will begin to overflow along the edge in contact with the mesh. When it is on the point of overflowing across the whole width, it is time to begin the stroke. This should go straight up the screen from bottom to top in one unhurried sweep. The art is to keep the scraping edge pressed firmly into the mesh and to see that the coating liquid is just overflowing all the way up. At the end of the stroke the screen is immediately lowered to a horizontal position, propped clear of the table and left to dry.

Ready-made coating troughs can be bought from the suppliers of screen process equipment or they can be improvised at home. Aluminium angle strip with a section measuring 1 in. × 1 in. or $1\frac{1}{2}$ in. × $1\frac{1}{2}$ in. is easily worked with simple hand tools. A trough to coat the whole screen should measure about 2 in. less than the inside width of the frame. But as aluminium is so cheap and the construction so simple, it would be worth making several little troughs, down to about 2 in. long, for coating borders and small areas here and there.

Aluminium (aluminum) is a soft metal and when handling it particular care must be taken not to bend or notch the edge. If the edge is not perfectly straight and smooth, it will be impossible to lay on an even coating. If the edge feels sharp or jagged when bought, polish it carefully by honing up and down with a smooth stone. The ends of the trough can be closed with Scotch tape or masking tape. This will last well enough, and it can be stripped off when the trough comes up for washing. A permanent closure can be made with glass fibre or one of the metal-filled resin pastes sold in garages for small repairs. Both of these materials are available in miniature packs.

5 Printing tables

Screen printing is usually done at a table, and indeed the printing table is the most important piece of furniture in the workshop. It occupies the place where the press would stand in any other printing craft. For first attempts, an improvised working top can be set up on an ordinary kitchen table, but for serious work it is essential to have a table designed and built specifically for printing.

When designing a printing table, the first consideration is the kind of printing to be done. There are two main kinds:

1 Individual sheet

Where the printing is done on individual sheets, the table is built only slightly larger than the screen frame. The frame is attached to the table by a hinge mechanism so that it can be raised and lowered always in the same spot, like the lid of a desk. The unprinted sheets are stacked up on one side, fed to the screen one by one, and then carried off to the drying rack.

2 Continuous length

Where textiles or wallpaper are to be printed, the table has to be a long one. Ideally it should be long enough for the whole piece of material to be spread out flat along its top in one continuous length. The screen is not attached to the table, but is free to move. Printing begins at one end and proceeds up the material step by step. The printed length is then left where it is on the table until dry.

This is a fundamental distinction. There is no reason why an artist printer should not attempt to work on both individual sheets and continuous length, but the two activities are quite different. And so is much of the equipment. For this reason the two kinds of table will be described separately. First, the table for printing individual sheets.

A comfortable working height is 34 in.; for children, 31 in. would be better. It is a mistake to have the table too low. The working top is the bed on which the sheet is laid while the print is being made, and it must be perfect. It must be solid, flat, hard, smooth and easily cleaned, and it must always be kept clean. The best tops are made of $\frac{3}{4}$ in. blockboard with a surface of laminated plastic sheet such as Formica.

A less expensive top can be made from $\frac{1}{8}$ in. hardboard tacked or glued to a solid wood bench. The top surface may be horizontal like an ordinary table, or inclined like a school desk, dropping from back to front at an angle of about 10°. When it comes to printing, the inclined top will be found to have several practical advantages; for instance, the printing colour will be less likely to drain down to the back and overflow at the hinges every time the screen is raised.

The simplest device for holding the screen in a raised position is a little wooden strut screwed to the side of the frame somewhere near the printer's left hand. When the screen is raised, the strut hangs down and rests against the working top. Drill a generous hole in the strut so that it can swing freely. Another good system used on large screens in old-fashioned print works is the hoist. A strong cord runs from the front corners of the frame, up over a couple of pulleys in the ceiling, and then down to a counterbalance weight. The machine-made outfits used by professional printers today have counterbalance weights incorporated in the hinge mechanism. Most specialist suppliers offer a hinge assembly of this kind as a separate item in their lists.

All hinges open and shut, but the screen printer expects his to do more than that. They must:

1 Take apart, so that the screen can be removed from the bed without undoing screws.
2 Open and shut precisely, with no slack or side play.
3 Allow for a certain adjustment of position; up, down, left, right, forward, back.
All this can be done in a very simple way.

Most large and well-stocked ironmongers and hardware stores carry a type of hinge called a loose pin butt (in the US a push-pin hinge). When the pin is withdrawn, the hinge comes apart. These hinges come in lengths from 2 in. to 4 in.: they are just what the amateur screen printer wants.

A good pair of hinges should have no slack. If there is any, the side play can be minimized by setting the hinges as far apart as possible, that is by hinging the screen on its long side. The hinges are not fastened direct to the printing bed itself, but to a separate strip of wood known as the hinge bar. The up, down, and sideways adjustments are allowed for in the special way the hinge bar is attached to the bed.

This is the method. Drill a $\frac{1}{2}$ in. hole down through the hinge bar about 2 in. from each end. Clamp the hinge bar temporarily in its correct position at the back of the printing bed, insert the $\frac{1}{2}$ in. bit in the holes in the hinge bar, and prick the centre of each hole in the surface of the bed underneath. Change to a $\frac{1}{4}$ in. bit, set it in the centres you have just pricked, and drill right down through the bed. Take two $\frac{1}{4}$ in. coach bolts, $\frac{1}{2}$ in. longer than the thickness of the bed and hinge bar combined. Insert them in the $\frac{1}{4}$ in. holes on the underside of the bed, and drive them up until they emerge through the hinge bar. Clean the chaff from the thread with a wire brush, apply a drop of oil, and slip on a large plain washer, a spring washer, another plain washer, and finally a wing nut. Remove the clamps.

The free play permitted by a $\frac{1}{4}$ in. bolt passing through a $\frac{1}{2}$ in. hole gives plenty of lateral adjustment. Vertical adjustment is made by slacking off the wing nuts and packing the space between the underside of the hinge bar and the bed. This is necessary when thick material is being printed. If $\frac{1}{8}$ in. board is being printed, a scrap of the same material is wedged under the hinge bar, and the wing nuts then tightened down hard.

The hinge bar is really an extension of the bed, and is never removed from it. The screens are brought up one at a time, connected to the hinge bar for the duration of the printing run, and then taken off again. All the preliminary work of stencil making, the cleaning up and storage takes place elsewhere. Even the smallest establishment is likely to have a number of screens lined up and waiting a turn to be printed. It would be a great convenience if, when the time came, each in turn could be slotted into position on the same hinge bar and fixed with the same pair of pins. As the hinges are machine-made, identical and interchangeable, this is a simple operation.

Take one hinge, remove the pin, and take the hinge apart. Set the two parts out in the correct position near the ends of the hinge bar, and screw them down permanently. Bring up a screen and lay it on the bed in the printing position, with the far edge pressed up

Fig 8 Adjustable hinge bar, section

against the two parts of the first hinge. Now remove the pin from a second hinge, take it apart, and fit the two parts into the corresponding spaces in the parts of the first hinge. Insert the two pins. The two hinges have now exchanged parts, but they have ended up as they began, two complete hinges. Screw the flaps of the second hinge to the screen frame. They can be left on it throughout its working life. Whenever a new screen is to be added, it is only necessary to buy one more hinge, remove the pin, take apart, and connect up with the original hinge on the hinge bar. In this way every screen in the studio can be made to slot into the same position. And, incidentally, it will be noticed that one spare pin is gained with every hinge bought. Pins are always getting lost, and it is just as well to have a reserve supply.

Where it is not possible to keep one table exclusively for printing, a portable top can be made from $\frac{1}{8}$ in. hardboard. Plywood with a laminated plastic surface is better, but heavier and much more expensive. The portable top can be fitted with an adjustable hinge bar.

The table for printing textiles or wallpaper is an entirely different piece of furniture. It has to be at least a yard longer than the longest piece of material likely to be printed. In the trade the tables often exceed a hundred yards in length. An amateur would probably be content with a table long enough to print one dress length. The table must be at least 12 in.

Fig 9 Adjustable hinge bar, viewed from above

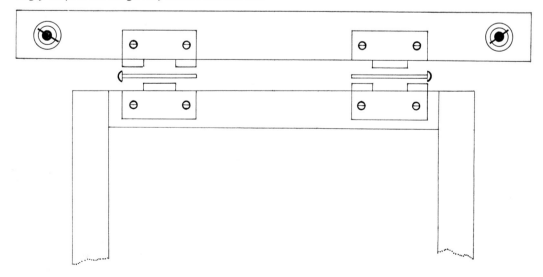

wider than the material to be printed; 4 ft is a reasonable width. Pulling a squeegee across such a width is quite a stretch, and to make the work as easy as possible the top should not be too high; 30 in. is about right.

A good working top can be made from $\frac{3}{4}$ in. or 1 in. blockboard, chipboard or ply. These all come in standard sheets measuring 4 ft × 8 ft: two sheets end to end would make a useful table. These sheets are inclined to sag after a time unless supported underneath by a solid framework of timber or closely spaced angle iron. A farmhouse kitchen table makes an excellent base on which to build.

Glue and screw a strip of 2 in. × 1 in. deal to the underside of the blockboard so as to strengthen the edges all the way round. Pad the top with one thickness of laundry felt or wool carpet underfelt stretched tight and tacked all round. Latex foam sheeting is not good enough for this purpose. Cover the underfelt with waterproof sheeting stretched tight and tacked all round. Ordinary polythene (polyethylene) sheeting may be used as a makeshift cover, but for heavy wear and a long and trouble-free life, it is worth buying one of the special waterproof 'topskins' manufactured for the trade. These consist of a plastic or vulcanised rubber coating bonded to a woven textile base. Several widths are available: the 52 in. width is just right for tacking to a table 48 in. wide.

The finished top should always be treated with respect. It should be washed down and mopped dry after every printing session. Glue and lacquer should not be spilled on it, hot irons should not be put down on it, pins and knives should not be allowed near it. At all times when not being used for printing, it should be covered with a sheet of hardboard.

6 Registration: 1

Armed with a screen and a squeegee, a table and a pot of colour, the beginner is almost fully equipped to start printing. Almost, but not quite. The one thing missing is some means of controlling the position in which the print will fall on the sheet. To a printer, this control of position is known as registration.

No printer can afford to underrate the importance of this part of his craft; it is one of the essential skills. Without it, all printing must be random; all attempts to print an edition, to print a repeating pattern, or to print any kind of work in more than one colour are doomed to failure. Success is largely a matter of technique, that is, knowing how to proceed. The present chapter deals with the technique of registering individual sheets.

Stripped down to essentials, registration consists of:

1 A device to fix the position of the screen.
2 A device to fix the position of the sheet in relation to the screen.

A well-made screen hinged at the back will fall every time in exactly the same spot. If the screen is connected to an adjustable hinge bar, the printer has all he needs.

The position of the sheet to be printed could be marked on the printing bed by drawing a pencil line round it. All the other sheets could then be laid in this rectangle one after the other. But this is a slow and uncertain method. The best way is to build an arrangement of jigs or guides around the sheet, and attach them to the bed with some kind of temporary adhesive. The stops need not enclose the sheet on all four sides; it is enough if they support two sides, one long, one short, making between them a right-angled corner. The printer then feeds each sheet into the corner until he can feel it butting up against the stops. This method is both accurate and quick.

The simplest kind of stop is made from a strip of cardboard. The cardboard should be about $\frac{1}{16}$ in. thicker than the paper on which the edition is to be printed. Three or four strips will be needed, each measuring 2 in. × 1 in. or thereabouts. Two are set against one of the long sides of the sheet, as far apart as possible, one or two against one of the short sides. Each one must make a perfect edge-to-edge contact with the sheet. The reliability of these stops depends on the care devoted to setting them up. Set them up one at a time, and fasten down to the printing base with a temporary adhesive.

Stops should never be fastened to the bed with nails, tacks, or hard-setting glue. At the end of the printing run they will be peeled off, and the bed must be left clean and smooth ready for the next job. During its working life the bed will have hundreds if not thousands of stops glued to it and taken off again. Whatever adhesive is used must be quick-setting, strong, and yet easily removed. Most printers use a latex adhesive or rubber cement. The stops can also be fastened down with straps of adhesive tape.

When printing on thick cardboard or plywood, the stops are usually made from a few offcuts of the same material. When printing on thin and flimsy material it is difficult to prevent the sheets from sailing over the top of the ordinary cardboard stop. In such cases it is better to use a stop in the form of a flap.

The best material for making this kind of stop is thin brass foil or 'shim'. This is stocked by non-ferrous metal merchants, engineers' suppliers, sculpture supply stores and hardware stores. It comes in the form of continuous strip 6 in. wide, and in various thicknesses: it costs very little. A suitable thickness would be 0·004 in. (four thousandths), and this can be cut easily with ordinary scissors. For each stop cut a strip measuring about $1\frac{1}{2}$ in. × $\frac{1}{2}$ in. Fold the strip over at a line half an inch in from one end, so as to make a little hinge with one flap twice as long as the other. Take one of the sheets of paper on which the edition is to be printed, and lay it on the bed. Set the stop against the edge of the sheet in such a way that the long flap goes underneath and the short flap on top. Press in until the edge of the paper makes positive contact with the inside of the fold in the brass strip. Fasten the short flap to the printing bed with a strap of adhesive tape. Lift the edge of the paper carefully so as to uncover the long flap. Fasten down the long flap with plenty of straps of adhesive tape. These brass stops are set up in the same position as the cardboard stops, that is, two against one of the long sides of the sheet of paper, one or two against one of the short sides.

Some printers use flaps made of masking tape or gummed paper strip, but neither of these materials can be trusted to keep its shape for long. As printing proceeds, the flap gets progressively weaker, the line of the fold becomes vague, and gradually drifts away from its original setting. This is an insidious source of error. It is not easy to see what is happening, and the trouble may be far advanced before the printer becomes aware that something is wrong.

When we speak of an edition, what we mean is a set of identical prints on identical sheets of paper. Everything depends on the paper being accurately cut and, unfortunately, this is something that cannot always be taken for granted. The manufacturer's guillotine will have cut all the sheets the same, but it may not have cut them with right angles in all four corners. Before starting to print, the printer should examine his stock of paper, and if there is only one good corner, he must go to the trouble of marking it on every sheet with a faint pencil cross. He will then be able to see that the good corner goes into the register stops each time. When counting out the paper, always allow seven or eight spare sheets.

These will be used as controls to check the accuracy of the registration; they will not be included in the edition proper.

A point of pride in all fine printing is the beautiful placing of the printed image on the sheet. This is achieved by careful planning; it cannot be left to chance. Two things are needed:

1 One of the control sheets of paper on which the edition is to be printed.

2 The artist's original master drawing.

A master drawing shows what the final print will look like. It will be used later on as the source from which the stencil will be made, but for the moment it is being used simply as an aid to fixing the position of the print on the sheet. The master drawing may be on any sort of paper and any shape or size, provided it is smaller than the control sheet. Lay the master drawing on the control sheet. Spend some time arranging it carefully, check the alignment and measure the margins, because the position decided on now is the position on which the prints will fall when the edition is run off. Fix the master drawing to the control sheet with tape or gum, and do not remove it until the edition is printed. If the master drawing is too valuable to be treated in this way, make a tracing of it and use that instead.

Designs containing more than one colour need a little more preparation. The intersecting lines of latitude and longitude form a grid by means of which the navigator can establish and check his position. Borrowing the same idea, the screen printer navigates with the aid of a grid, abbreviated in his case to four little crosses drawn in the margin of the master drawing just outside the picture space, one cross at each corner. The crosses are called register marks. They will be referred to constantly in the course of making the stencils and fitting the separate colours together. They should be drawn very neatly in Indian ink, using a ruler and a fine ruling pen.

Fig 10 Register marks

So much for the preparation. The next job is to transfer the image from the master drawing to the screen in the form of a stencil. There are many different ways of doing this, and they will be described in detail in later chapters. But whichever method is used, the register marks must always be included in the stencil. Where the design consists of more than one colour printing, each separate colour will need its own stencil. If there are plenty of screens, it saves time to give each stencil a screen to itself, but the same screen can be used for them all, one after the other, provided it is cleaned thoroughly in between each stencil and the next.

Stencil making is normally carried out away from the printing table; it may be in a photographic darkroom or in some other building altogether. Indeed there is no need to go near the printing table until the stencil is complete and the screen ready for printing. When this point has been reached, only one problem remains to be solved: how to find where to put the register stops on the printing bed.

This is the way. Connect the screen to the hinge bar. Lay the master drawing on the printing bed. It will be remembered that the master drawing is still mounted in the carefully chosen position on the control sheet. Lower the screen into contact with the master drawing. All types of stencil are more or less translucent and, by peering through, it should be possible to see the drawing underneath. Shift the drawing about until it coincides with the image on the screen. The true position will show itself without any doubt when the Indian ink crosses come directly under the cross-shaped openings in the stencil. This position must now be fixed.

Hold everything down by pressing on the centre of the mesh with the palm of the left hand. Insert a thin steel rule or long palette knife under the mesh and on top of the master drawing. Hold the drawing down with the palette knife. Take away the left hand and lift the screen. Place a heavy weight in the centre of the drawing or, better still, fasten it down temporarily with tape. The register stops can now be set up at leisure against the edges of the control sheet on which the master drawing is mounted.

For his first attempts at printing an edition, the beginner should keep to one colour. Concentrate on achieving technical perfection: let us make it twelve perfectly placed identical prints. The accuracy of the placing can be tested in this way. Take a few spare prints. When these are dry, put them back in the register stops and print on them again. There should be no double image. If there is a double image, try to find the cause, and put it right. It is no use continuing in the hope that things will come right by themselves; they will not. The importance of perfect registration cannot be exaggerated. Any scheme of printing in more than one colour must rest on a solid foundation. If the first colour is printed all over the place, it is absurd to expect the subsequent colours to fit.

When printing an edition in more than one colour, this is the procedure. Take the seven or eight spare sheets that have been set aside as controls, and print on them colour NO. 1, complete with register marks in the corners. These prints will be used to check the fitting of all the subsequent colours; they are guides for the printer, not for publication. Now, with screen filler or masking tape, cover up the register marks in the stencil so that they will not appear on the prints of the edition. Print the edition in the first colour. Remove the screen, remove the register stops, clean up the bed.

Bring up the screen carrying the stencil of colour NO. 2, and connect to the hinge bar. Lay the master drawing on the bed and shift it about until the register marks coincide. When the true position has been found, set up the register stops in the usual way. Remove the master drawing. As a second check, take one of the colour NO. 1 control prints complete with register marks, and set it in the register stops. Lower the screen and peer through. If colour NO. 1 happens to be a very pale colour, it may be difficult to decide whether the crosses are fitting or not. In this case, mix up a batch of printing colour NO. 2, load up the screen and make a trial print, complete with register marks, on to the control print of colour NO. 1. This will show conclusively the accuracy of the fit.

If the register marks fit, well and good: we can be sure that the print itself will be in register. If they don't, stop and find the cause of the trouble. It is fatally easy at this moment to make a hasty adjustment that can only lead to a greater error when it comes to fitting the remaining colours. At this stage the error is not likely to be greater than the thickness of a pencil line. To make this correction, slack off the wing nuts and use the adjustable hinge bar. Do not on any account disturb the register stops. If a correction has been necessary, take a test print on one of the control sheets. Finally, cover up the register marks in the stencil so that they will not appear in the prints of the edition. Print the edition in the second colour. Remove the screen, remove the register stops, clean up the bed.

The same procedure is followed with all the remaining colours.

One thing emerges clearly from this account of registration: the large number of separate stages through which the work has to be nursed on its way from the original drawing to the finished print. Error can creep in at every stage, and the greater the number of colours in the print, the greater the hazard. Even when every care has been taken, there is likely to be a small irreducible error. This will show itself in the print at any place where two colours come together in a line of edge-to-edge contact. One of three things might happen:

1 The two colours might meet perfectly.
2 They might overlap.
3 There might be a gap of white paper showing between the two colours.

The white gap must be prevented at all costs. This is done by giving the stencil of the first colour a little extra width, so that it encroaches on the territory of the second colour by about one-sixteenth of an inch. The stencil of the second colour keeps to the true line as given by the master drawing. In the print there will thus be a narrow band where colour NO. 2 overlaps colour NO. 1, but this is better than showing a gap of white paper.

7 Registration: 2

Nobody who has ever tried to design a repeating pattern needs reminding that this is a special problem. The answer is not to be found in tracing paper; it is not as easy as that. What is called for is the ability to think and to see and to organize ideas within the beat of a regular rhythm. The underlying rhythm is always represented by a grid of parallel lines intersecting at right angles like the lines of latitude and longitude. Each intersection marks the centre of gravity of one unit of the repeat. If we travel along any of the grid lines from one intersection to the next, we will have travelled from the centre of one unit of the repeat to the centre of its next recurrence.

This is exactly what happens when it comes to printing a repeating pattern. The grid is first set out on the designer's master drawing, and from here it is projected on to the surface of the material to be printed. By means of a system of register marks, the screen is guided along the lines of the grid from one intersection to the next, and at each intersection it is lowered into position and prints one unit of the repeat.

The master drawing must be large enough to include one unit of the repeat drawn full size, and all around it a sufficient number of neighbouring units to show how the repeat will develop. Particular attention must be paid to the line where the units fit together. This is a line of natural weakness, and every mistake will show up here. The lines of the grid must be drawn in very accurately with a fine ruling pen: they will be referred to at every stage of the process, and they must be absolutely dependable. Some mark should also be made to show the north-south east-west orientation of the drawing. Without this, it is only too easy at a later stage to make a mistake and find that the pattern is running across the material instead of up and down.

When the master drawing is quite perfect, stencil making can go ahead. Each colour will need a stencil to itself and this really means a screen to itself. The various methods of stencil making are described in later chapters, but not all of them are suitable for repeat pattern work. The colours used for printing textiles and wallpaper will eat through or lift off about half the available stencil materials, and only the most resistant and durable kinds can be used. These stencils are difficult if not impossible to remove from the mesh, and it may not be worth while even to make the attempt. In effect, the printer has this choice:

1 Regard the mesh as expendable, and destroy it at the end of the run. With a cotton mesh, printing a one-off length, this is probably the best solution.

2 With a nylon or polyester mesh, wash out the printing colour at the end of the run, and store the stencil, mesh and screen intact for future use. This presupposes plenty of screen frames and storage space. If the design is a very popular one, and hundreds of yards of printing are expected of it, possibly in a range of different colours, this may well be the best solution.

3 Use a nylon or polyester mesh, and keep to those types of stencil that are known to come away satisfactorily at the end.

Whatever kind of stencil is used, register marks must be included. They are traced up from the grid lines on the master drawing.

The next job is to project the grid on to the material to be printed. In practice this can be done in two different ways, according to whether the printer is working with small screens or large. Amateurs usually learn the craft on small screens, because they are easier to manage in every way than large screens. So let us begin with small screens.

We will suppose a small design fitting on to a simple square grid with lines spaced 9 in. apart both ways. To take a print measuring 9 in. × 9 in. in comfort, the screen should measure not less than 12 in. × 16 in. It is worth noting that the area of the screen is considerably larger than the area of the print. Make the stencil, complete with register marks, and when the screen is ready for printing lower it on to the master drawing so that the register marks coincide with the lines of the grid. This position must now be fixed. Place a

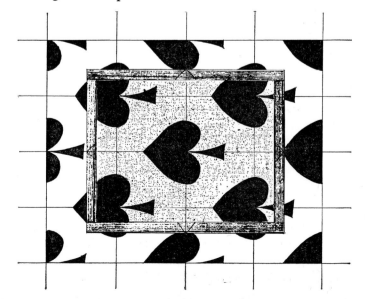

Fig 11 Repeat pattern grid

heavy weight inside the screen to prevent it from moving about and then, with Indian ink and a fine ruling pen, draw a vertical line on the outside of the screen frame at the four points where the grid lines pass through. These sight marks will be used as guides throughout the printing.

The material to be printed must be stretched out hard and flat and straight, and fastened to the top of the long printing table. This is really a two-man job, but the following method can be recommended to printers working on their own.

Materials

        2 rough wood strips measuring 48 in. long, 2 in. × 1 in. in section.

        4 3in. G clamps.

        10 drawing pins or thumb tacks.

        1 roll ⅝in. Scotch tape or masking tape.

Method

Spread out the material with the selvedges parallel with the sides of the table. Lay the wood strips across, one at each end. Fasten one end of the material to its wood strip with five of the drawing pins (thumb tacks), and clamp the ends of the wood to the edges of the table. Tack the free end of the material to the second wood strip, and pull as hard as possible to stretch the material. Keep the material stretched, and clamp the ends of the second wood strip to the edges of the table. Stick down the two selvedges with tape, release the clamps, and remove the wood strips. Stick down the two ends of the material with tape.

For the finest registration, it is not quite enough to tape the selvedges; the whole width of the material has to be stuck down. To do this we can coat the table top with one of the modern temporary adhesives. These substances, always known as Permanent adhesives, consist of a creamy solution of a plastic polymer designed for application by scraper or squeegee. Using 3 oz per square yard or thereabouts, spread the adhesive in a perfectly even thin film, and leave to dry. Since drying takes several hours, working time will be saved if the table can be coated the evening before the material is to be laid down. This kind of adhesive dries with a permanently tacky surface. It will hold any paper or textile pressed against it, and yet leave no trace of itself on the back. Up to twenty lengths of material can be laid on the table one after the other before the film of adhesive needs to be renewed.

The next job is to work out how many times the unit of the repeat will fit into the width of the material. Let us suppose the material to be 36 in. wide: our 9 in. units will fit into this width exactly four times. If the material had been 40 in. wide, our units would go four times and a bit over. It is very awkward to see a line of complete units running down one selvedge, and a line of half units running down the other. The only satisfactory solution is to arrange the grid centrally, so that any incomplete units are shared equally between the two selvedges. Go to the ends of the material and make a pencil tick to mark the centre point. Measuring outwards from here, make ticks to mark the ends of the long lines of the grid. Join up the ticks with a faint pencil line running right down the material. If the material is not longer than about twelve feet a straight piece of pine can be used as a ruler. Lines longer than twelve feet can be put in by the builders' line method.

Take a builders' line, that is, a length of thin flax twine, and ask a helper to hold one end. Walk backwards away from him, keeping the line taut and rubbing charcoal or coloured chalk into it until it is thoroughly coated. Hold the ends of the twine down on the ticks marking the ends of the long grid lines, and pull as tight as possible. Now with the free hand reach out, lift the twine vertically like a bowstring, and let it snap back on to the table. The result will be a perfectly straight chalk dust line.

In our example the grid lines running across the material are also spaced 9 in. apart. Measure out these spaces and mark them in pencil on one of the selvedges. Draw the lines across the material with the help of a large set square held against the selvedge. The grid is now complete.

A moment ago, attention was drawn to the obvious fact that the area of the screen is larger than the area of the unit printed by it. The significance of this becomes clear as soon as we start to print. We cannot begin at one end and then go straight up the material printing units 1, 2, 3, 4, 5, just like that. Lowering the screen into position NO. 2 would mean partly overlapping the freshly printed unit at position NO. 1. The wet colour would be picked up by the underside of the screen and transferred in due course to the material as an offset print. The only way to avoid this trouble is to work up the material printing units 1, 3, 5, 7, 9, and then, when these are dry, returning to fill in units 2, 4, 6, 8, 10.

It is possible to print small screens single handed, but very much easier and quicker for two people working together as a team, printer and helper facing each other across the table. The screen is lowered into the correct position at each intersection of the grid by watching the sight marks drawn in Indian ink on the outside of the frame. Both printer and helper take a hand in the printing. The squeegee is pulled from one to the other across the table and then back again, making two strokes for each print. The one who is not pulling the squeegee holds the screen steady.

This method brings repeat pattern printing well within the scope of the textile designer working at home or in school. It is not possible to work with simpler equipment than this. Fine registration should not be expected, and when making stencils it would be wise to allow a generous margin of deliberate overlap.

The equipment used by professional printers is designed for rapid printing combined with accurate registration. Grid lines are not drawn on the material. Registration is controlled from the side of the table by means of a steel guide rail and a set of adjustable register stops. The screens are normally 12 in. longer than the width of the material to be printed.

As always, the starting point is a master drawing based on a grid. To illustrate the technique of registration with the small screen, we used an imaginary drawing based on a simple 9 in. square grid, and a piece of material measuring 36 in. wide. A large screen can accommodate without any difficulty a printing area measuring 36 in. × 18 in., that is a block of eight 9 in. units. With a large screen this block can be printed as quickly as the small screen can print a single 9 in. square, and this means that printing is eight times as fast.

But the real difference between the two methods is the use of the steel guide rail in preference to the grid drawn on the material. The guide rail is a length of bright steel angle section measuring $1\frac{1}{2}$ in. × $1\frac{1}{2}$ in., securely fastened with bolts to the edge of the table, and running the whole length in one dead straight line. This is an expensive fixture, but essential for the finest registration. An excellent guide rail can be improvised by screwing a straight length of 2 in. × 1 in. softwood to the edge of the table. This is the cheapest way to learn the use of the guide rail and the technique of printing with large screens.

The guide rail provides the straight base line from which the whole work is set out. The lengths of the repeat are measured out along it, and their positions marked by register stops. The register stops used by professional printers consist of small metal blocks machined to fit like a saddle over the guide rail. They can be slid along to any desired position and then fixed by tightening a set screw. These stops can be bought from the specialist manufacturers. A large number will be needed, one for each position of the repeat. Amateurs working with a softwood guide rail should measure out the lengths of the repeat, prick a

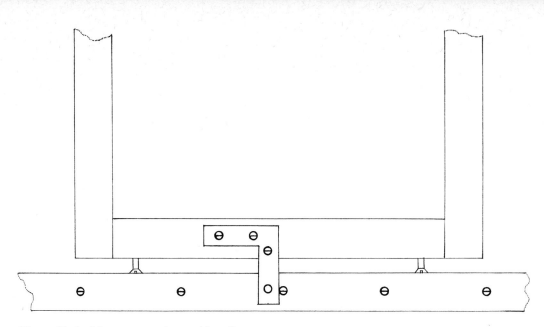

Fig 12 End of frame set against guide rail

hole as accurately as possible with a bradawl, and insert a $1\frac{1}{2}$ in.$\times 8$ wood screw at each position.

To complete the system, two temporary additions have to be made to the screen frame. These act as links between the frame and the guide rail.

The first of these provides a means of adjusting the axis of the screen relative to the guide rail. Two $1\frac{1}{2}$ in.$\times 8$ wood screws are set in the end frame of the screen projecting like the buffers of a locomotive. In its working position the screen rests on the table with the heads of these screws pressed up against the guide rail. Held in this way the screen can be moved along the table and the guide rail will keep it to a straight line. The centre line of the screen should make a right angle with the guide rail, indeed it must do so if it is to agree with the lines of the grid. If for any reason the centre line is inclined to the left or the right, this can be corrected by giving a half turn to one or other of the two screws in the end of the frame.

The second temporary addition is a 3 in.$\times 3$ in. steel angle plate screwed to the upper surface of the end frame of the screen in such a way that it projects over and beyond the guide rail. When it comes to printing, the screen is lowered into position with the edge of the angle plate pressed hard up against each register stop in turn, and the heads of the two adjustable screws pressed hard up against the guide rail.

The whole programme runs like this:

1 Make the stencil from the master drawing, placing it centrally in the screen, and with the lines of the grid correctly aligned with the axis of the screen. Include register marks.

2 Attach angle plate and adjustable screws to the end frame of the screen.

3 Lay the screen on the printing table with the heads of the screws pressed hard up against the guide rail. Adjust the screws if necessary to bring the axis of the stencil to a correct 90° with the guide rail.

4 Slide the master drawing under the screen and shift it about until the register marks coincide. Hold everything in this position whilst the next measurement is being taken.

5 Measure the space between the guide rail and the selvedge nearest to it, as shown on the master drawing. This space will vary slightly from one job to the next, but it is not likely to be less than about 8 in. as it has to include:

i The heads of the adjustable screws, say 1 in.
ii The thickness of the screen frame, say 2 in.
iii The width of the well, say 5 in.

6 Remove the screen and master drawing.

7 Using the measurement just found, draw a chalk line on the table top to mark the line of the selvedge.

8 Stretch the material and fasten it down, with the selvedge set to the chalk line.

9 Lay the screen on the end of the material in the position where print NO. 1 will be made.

10 Bring the first register stop into contact with the edge of the angle plate, and fix it there.

11 From this stop, space out all the other stops at the length of the repeat, and fix them in position.

12 Mask out the register marks on the stencil. Recruit a helper. Load the screen with colour and make a couple of trial prints on a scrap of waste material.

13 Print positions 1, 3, 5, 7, 9 on the material itself. When the colour is dry, fill in positions 2, 4, 6, 8, 10.

14 Remove the angle plate and adjustable screws. Wash up the screen.

It is possible to combine the advantages of the small screen with the advantages of the guide rail. All that is required is a large T-square specially constructed to carry the small screen. The head of the T-square takes the place of the end frame of a large screen. It should be made from a straight piece of 2 in. × 2 in. softwood, about two feet long, and fitted with a pair of adjustable screws and a steel angle plate. The arm of the T-square should be long enough to span the whole width of the table.

Stretch the material and fasten it down with the selvedge parallel with the guide rail and spaced about eight inches away from it. Lay the master drawing on the end of the material in the position where print NO. 1 will be made. Make sure that it is centrally placed, and that the grid is correctly aligned with the selvedge. Tape it temporarily in this position. Lay the screen on the master drawing and move it about until the register marks coincide. Place a heavy weight inside the screen to hold it in this position. Bring up the long T-square so that the arm rests against the side frame of the screen, and the heads of the adjustable screws are in contact with the guide rail. Clamp the screen to the arm with a couple of G-clamps. Set up the first register stop in contact with the angle plate, and space out all the others according to the length of the repeat.

If the screen can only print a 9 in. square, and the material is 36 in. wide, this will mean four trips up the table in parallel lanes running side by side. The register stops on the guide rail will hold good throughout, but the screen frame will have to be shifted up the arm of the T-square to a fresh starting position at the head of each lane. The exact position can be found every time by consulting the master drawing.

The great advantage of this method is that there is no need to mark the material with pencil lines.

8 Furniture and equipment

Intrepid and resourceful screen printers have been known to set up and practice their craft in cellars, in bedrooms, in the corners of potteries and carpenters' shops, but this has been from necessity and not from choice. Given the choice, screen printing should have a room, or even a chain of rooms, to itself. The ideal workshop would be housed in a new building with heating, lighting, plumbing and ventilation designed by the printer in consultation with the architect. More often it is a case of adapting part of an existing building. The room selected for adaptation need not be at ground level, since none of the equipment is heavy.

What is important is that the accommodation should be tall, airy and well ventilated. Natural ventilation should be supplemented if necessary by extractor fans. Some of the printing colours and solvents give off fumes which tend to hang about in the air. In a confined space this is not only unpleasant for the printer; a concentration of fumes slows down the drying of the printed material. All the solvents used by the screen printer have a flash point above 90°F, and so they lie safely outside the restrictions of the Cellulose Regulations and the Petroleum Act (in the UK). Nevertheless, fire is a risk in any workshop using volatile solvents, and ordinary care should be taken to prevent and deal with an outbreak.

When planning the workshop, the best layout is one which follows the natural sequence of operations through the craft; at one end the preparation of the master drawing, at the other end the drying of the finished prints. As far as possible the space should be divided into territories. Within each territory will be installed the electrical supply points, water supply, drainage, working surface and storage for one particular part of the craft. It should not be necessary to go to the paint cupboard to get at the photographic chemicals.

The studio end of the workshop should contain the usual drawing office furniture and equipment: an inclined stand to take a large drawing board, an adjustable lamp, a high stool, a large plan chest for storing paper.

Stencil making can be divided into three categories: serigraphic, knife-cut, photographic. Serigraphic artists need a good working top surfaced with hardboard or white Formica. The same top can also be used for knife-cut stencils. For the finest registration a special tracing table should be made, illuminated from below by a bank of diffused electric lights. The top should consist of a sheet of $\frac{1}{4}$ in. plate glass frosted on the underside. When the stencils have been cut, they have to be stuck to the screen. There is a dry way and a wet way of doing this. The dry way needs a thermostatically controlled electric iron, the wet way needs an electric fan. The next chapter explains in detail.

Photographic stencil making can be done in almost any clean, dust-free place sheltered from the direct rays of the sun. Many of the modern proprietary coatings will tolerate leisurely handling in indirect light, and for them a darkroom is a luxury but not a necessity. The essential fixtures are:

1 A flat-topped work bench surfaced with white Formica. Under this bench can be housed the rolls of proprietary coated paper, a nest of large photographic dishes, funnels, rubber gloves, squeegees, coating troughs, cleaning rags, photographic chemicals, thermometer, scales and liquid measures.

2 The exposure lamp and contact printing frame. These two together form the centre-piece of the photographic department. An excellent and very simple arrangement is to lay the contact printing frame face up on the table, and suspend the lamp from the ceiling above it. This equipment will be described in detail in the chapter on photographic stencil making.

3 A large, deep sink, and an abundant supply of hot and cold running water. There should be, if possible, a mixing tap with a length of flexible tubing and a fine rose. If this is not possible, a gardener's watering can with a fine rose will do the work just as well. Behind the sink should be a white Formica splashboard on which the stencil will be supported whilst it is being hosed. The lower edge of the splashboard should be set forward so that the rinsing water is shed into the sink. Powerful lights should be set up to illuminate the surface of the splashboard, because the stencil has to be examined closely all the time it is being hosed.

So much for the photographic equipment.

The paint cupboard will house the stock of colours and the thinners to go with them. The space should be divided into clearly labelled bays, so that the different groups of colours are kept apart. If this is not done, cans of oil colour will find their way into the shelf reserved for acrylics, and the result will be the ruination of a screen.

A mixing table with a washable top should stand nearby. Lying on top, always ready for use, will be a set of palette knives, their blades clean and bright.

To carry the colour from the mixing table to the printing table there is nothing better than one of those two-tiered trolleys sometimes known as tea waggons. The top tier carries the colour and the squeegee, the bottom tier carries all those things that might be needed for running repairs in the course of printing: rags and thinners to clear a clogged screen, masking tape and screen filler to patch up a leaking screen, a stack of old newspaper for mopping up.

Lengths of material printed with a repeating pattern are left to dry in position on the long table. Drying can be accelerated, if necessary, by the use of hot air fans. Wet prints on individual sheets of paper are much more of a problem: unless there is a rack ready to take them as they come from the screen, they are very easily spoiled. There are two types of rack:

1 *Farmhouse clothes airer type.* This is a framework suspended from the ceiling by ropes and pulleys. The frame consists of a set of 2 in. × 1 in. softwood rails running parallel and spaced about four inches apart. Small bulldog clips (clamps) are screwed to the rails at intervals of 8 in. or thereabouts. The bulldog clips hold the wet prints by the edge, two clips to each print. This rack should be installed within easy reach of the printing table.

2 *Horizontal tray type.* This is a stack of individual trays or frames, one tray to every print in the edition. Each tray is a flat rectangular framework with widely spaced strips of 1 in. × $\frac{1}{4}$ in. softwood nailed across it. The trays are stacked up in a vertical pile on the floor near the printing table. Just before printing is due to begin, the top tray is lifted off and laid on the floor next to the base of the stack. The first wet print is laid face up on this tray, and another empty tray is then brought down from the stack and laid on top of it. In this way the new pile grows, each print being separated from the next by one of the trays.

This is the original version of the horizontal tray drying rack. A luxurious all-steel, spring-loaded modern version can be ordered from the specialist suppliers.

Cleaning the screen is, without any doubt, the most unpopular part of the whole silk screen process. It comes at the end of the printing run when the printer is feeling tired and in no mood for this kind of work. And yet it is not a job that can be left until tomorrow. If the screen is washed straight away, the colour will come out easily; if it is left overnight it will set solid, and even the most powerful solvents may fail to clear it. Mesh materials are far too valuable to be squandered in this way.

The job can be made a lot easier if the proper facilities are available. These are:

1 A flat-topped cleaning bench larger than the largest screen in the workshop. The top should be surfaced with white Formica. Underneath should be kept a supply of cotton rags, old newspaper, offcuts of cardboard, a nylon scrubbing brush and a battery of solvents. A container for waste material should stand nearby.

2 A large deep sink with an abundant supply of hot and cold running water. A mixing tap is not necessary, but flexible tubing should be fitted to both hot and cold taps. The function of this sink is to de-grease the mesh by a process of rinsing and, if necessary, scrubbing with liquid detergents. No oily solvents will be used here. A white Formica splashboard, larger

than the largest screen in the workshop, should be fixed to the wall behind the sink. The lower edge should be set forward so that the rinsing water is shed into the sink. A little teak shelf, drilled with drainage holes, should be screwed with brass screws to the lower edge of the splashboard as a support for the screen frame. Two side panels should be added so as to form a small cubicle inside which vigorous hosing can take place without fear of drenching the rest of the workshop.

The whole of the cleaning area should be very well lit.

9 Stencil making: knife-cut stencils

The only tool needed for making a cut-paper stencil is a sharp-pointed knife. A surgeon's scalpel could be used, or any of the finely tempered model maker's knives. (In the US a simple stencil knife is used with a fixed or rotating swivel blade.) Professional stencil cutters use a length of $\frac{1}{8}$ in. silver steel rod with one end ground back for a distance of about an inch so as to form a thin, narrow blade. Viewed from the side, the blade comes to an acute point; the angle is somewhere between 30° and 45°. It takes a bit of time to get used to this tool. The art is to hold it perpendicular to the sheet of paper, and to steer it round curves by rolling the rod between the thumb and first two fingers. For practice, one of the best exercises is to try to cut round the headlines on a newspaper.

Whatever kind of knife is used, the blade must be kept as sharp as a razor. A blunt knife will only make a torn and ragged stencil. A fine grain stone should be kept on the bench, and the knife honed up and down on it once or twice in every working day. Most craftsmen have strong personal views on which is the best kind of stone; some prefer an oil stone such as Arkansas, others a water stone such as Water of Ayr. These are both excellent stones. But a warning must be given about oil. If the slightest trace gets on the hands it will soon

Fig 13 Knife-cut stencil in laminated sheet
One square, rotated and overprinted

1 Making the screen frame

2 The master frame

3 *opposite*
Mesh materials
Photomicrographs of
i silk bolting cloth
ii polyester multifilament
iii nylon monofilament

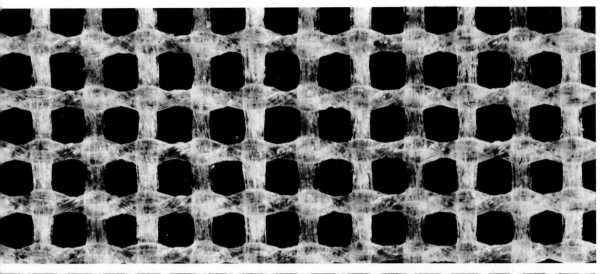

4 Liquid screen filler on cotton organdie, mesh count 96 threads to the inch
Photomicrograph by Gene Cox

5 Knife-cut stencil on cotton organdie, mesh count 96 threads to the inch
Photomicrograph by Gene Cox

6 A coated screen being exposed in a small contact frame

7 Mercury vapour lamp, vacuum frame and water jet filter pump

8 Coating a screen

9　The steel guide rail and register stops

10   Portable printing bed with adjustable hinge bar

11   All-steel hinge assembly with counterbalance weights
      A large frame is being used to carry a small screen

12 Print by schoolgirl,
age thirteen
Emulsion
colour, cotton
organdie screen

13 Print by housewife
Cut-paper
stencil, four
colour printings
in thin film inks

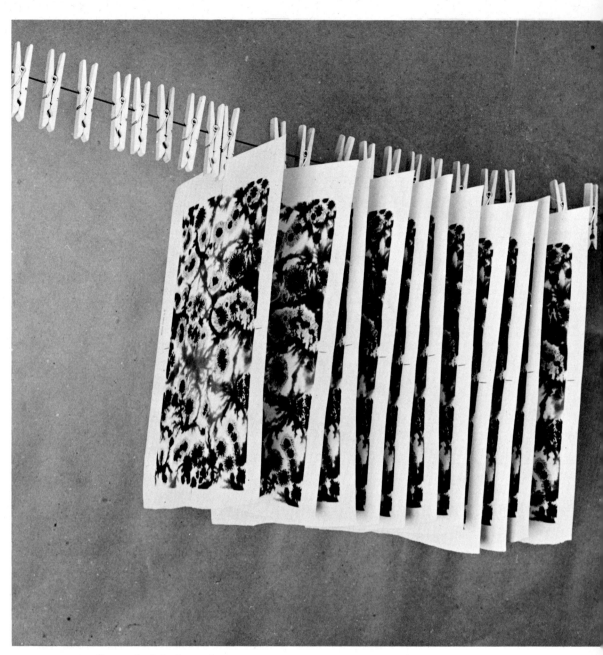

14   Improvised drying rack

15   All-steel drying rack

16 Stencil punched out of
    zinc sheet
    Yoruba, twentieth
    century

17 Screen printed electronic
    circuit (detail)

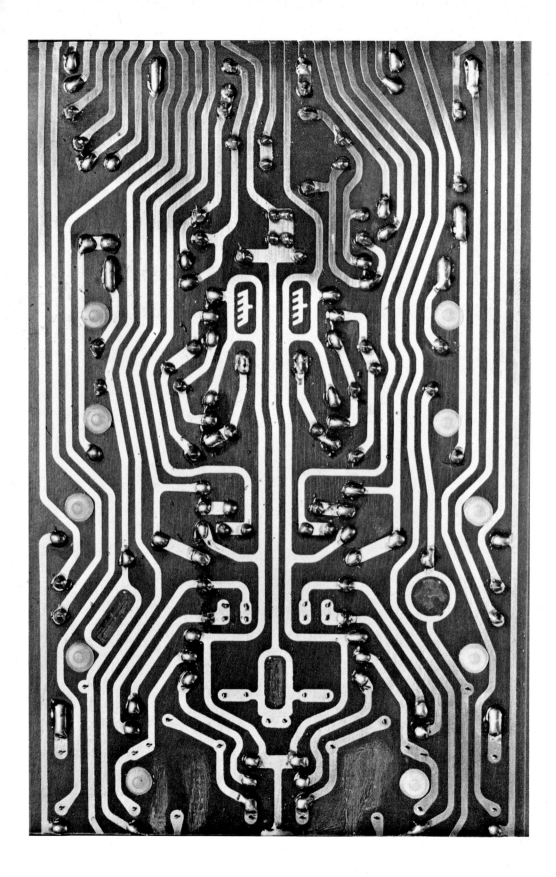

18   Calendar designed by Frank Humphris and printed in the Priestley Studios, Gloucester, in 1937
      Knife-cut stencils, ten colour printings

19   Illuminated panel on amusement machine
Ten colour printings on glass

20   Thick paper stencil, thick print in oil colour

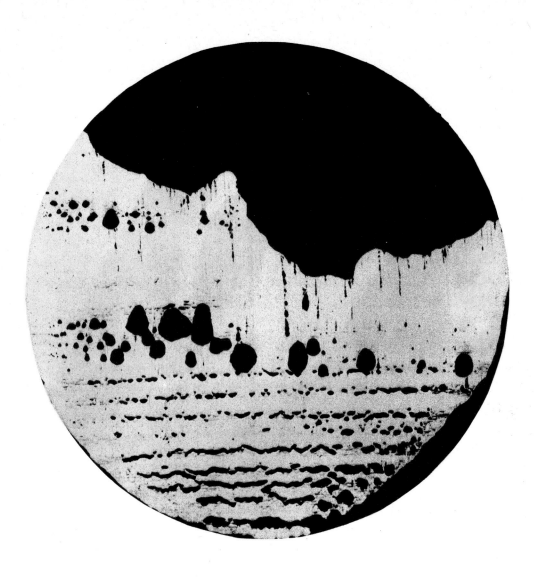

21　Painting with the squeegee

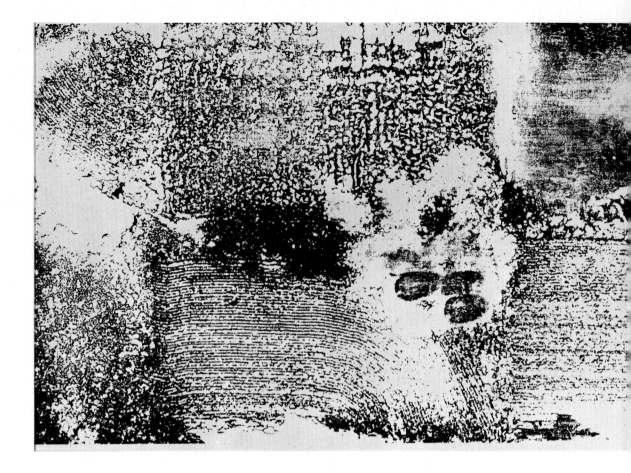

22　French chalk

23 Shellac liquid filler and some French chalk
Two colour printings in thickened textile dyes

T019401

24   Screen printed textile
Strawberry Hill designed by Ian Logan and screen printed on heavy cotton
for Parker-Knoll Textiles

25   Print by schoolgirl, age thirteen
Shellac liquid filler, two colour printings in emulsion colour

26 John Piper *Pen y Bont Congregational Church* 1966
97·5 × 68·6 cm
Marlborough Fine Art, London

27 Sidney Nolan *Kelly VI* 1965
77·5 × 58·1 cm
Marlborough Fine Art, London

28 Eduardo Paolozzi *Moonstrips Empire News. The Silken World of Michelangelo* 1967
38 × 25·5 cm
Editions Alecto, London

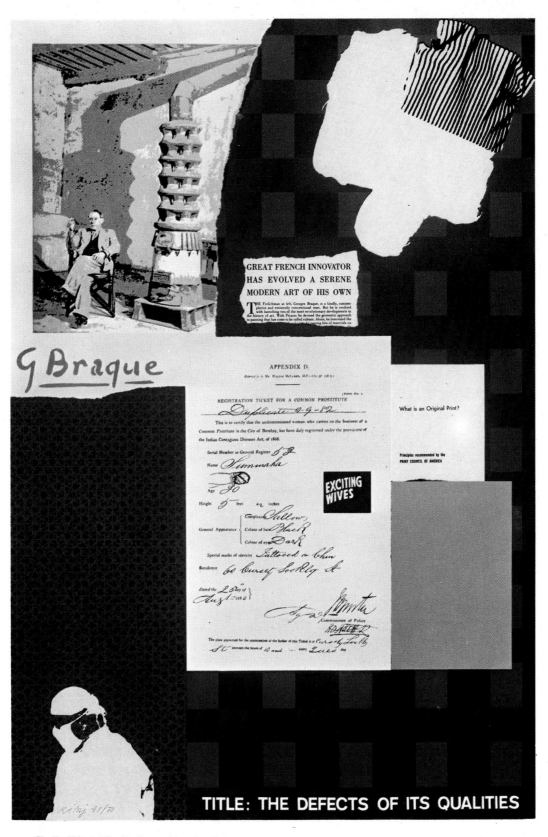

29 R. B. Kitaj *The Defects of its Qualities* 1967
90·2 × 60·9 cm
Marlborough Fine Art, London

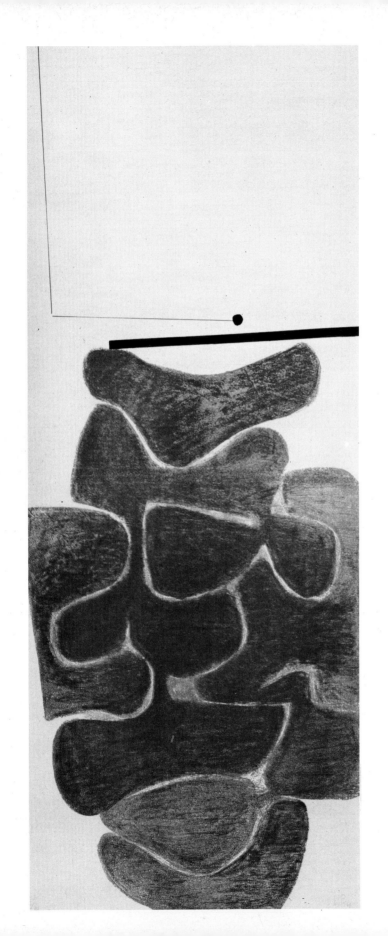

30 Victor Pasmore *Points of Contact No. 12* 1967
    109·8 × 44·5 cm
    Marlborough Fine Art, London

31 Harold Cohen *Richard V* 1967
    68·6 × 77·5 cm
    Marlborough Fine Art, London

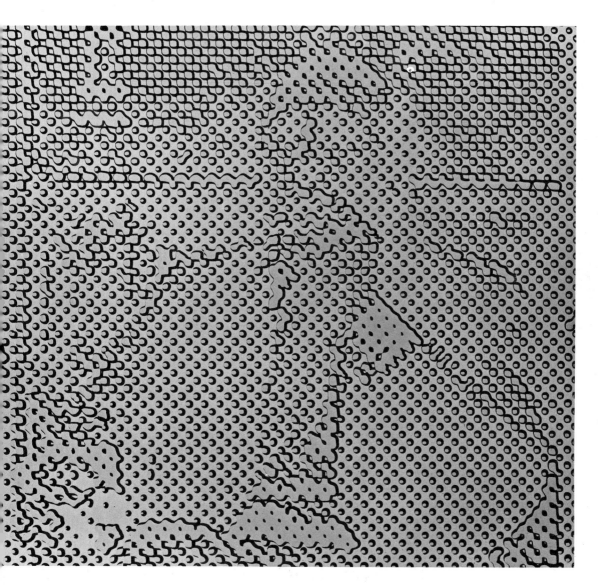

32 Jean Dubuffet *Banque de l'Hourloupe* 1967
    25 × 16·5 cm
    Editions Alecto, London

find its way to the stencil, and this can cause great trouble later on when the time comes to stick the stencil to the screen.

For serious work there really is no substitute for a stencil cutting knife, but for first attempts, for special effects, and for screen printing classes with junior children, something can be done with scissors or even with the bare hands. Surely there could be no simpler introduction to the craft than this.

Materials
small screen covered with organdie
squeegee
printing colour
stack of newsprint cut to the size of the screen

Method
Draw a simple shape in the middle of one of the sheets of paper, and tear or cut it out. Lay the paper stencil on one of the clean sheets of newsprint, lay the screen on top, load up with printing colour and make an out-and-back stroke with the squeegee. Lift the screen. If all has gone well, two things will have happened: the squeegee stroke will have made a print of the cut-out shape, and at the same time the printing colour will have stuck the paper stencil to the underside of the mesh. This is all there is to do: the screen is now ready for printing an edition.

All printing colours have this adhesive property to some extent. The so-called thin film inks will hold a stencil to the screen for over a hundred prints. The oil-in-water emulsion colours will hold until the paper becomes soggy; this may be after anything up to fifty prints, it depends on the paper.

The proprietary wax-impregnated stencil papers used by typists (mimeograph stencil) can be made to adhere to the screen just like any other paper stencil. This is particularly interesting because it means that the screen can be used to duplicate a typewritten stencil. But more than that, these stencil sheets can also take line drawings and stipple tints.

One of the attractions of all these simple methods is that the stencil comes away with the printing colour in the ordinary course of washing up, and the screen is immediately clear for the next job. With every other method a separate and often lengthy operation is needed to remove the stencil.

The usefulness of the cut-paper stencil is by no means limited to elementary exercises: it is quite capable of handling ambitious projects in several colours overprinted in register. If this is to be attempted there must be a master drawing complete with register marks, and a printing table fitted with an adjustable hinge bar. This is the procedure:

1 Make a tracing of the master drawing, and include on it the register marks and the outlines of all the separate areas of colour. Give the back of the tracing a good coating of red or black conté crayon or coloured chalk.
2 Lay the tracing on a sheet of stencil paper and fix it in place with drawing pins, thumb tacks or tape. With a ball-point pen, go over the register marks and the outlines of colour NO. I, so as to transfer them to the stencil paper.
3 Remove the tracing, and lay the stencil paper on a sheet of hardboard or plate glass. Cut round the outlines of colour NO. I. Any detached pieces, such as the centres of O's, should be numbered and kept in a little box for the time being.
4 Lay the tracing on the printing bed and fix it down with tape.
5 Arrange the cut-paper stencil on the tracing, positioning the detached pieces carefully.

6 Lower the screen.

7 With a stiff brush or the tip of a finger, apply a spot of fish glue (isenglass) through the mesh here and there, just sufficient to hold the various parts of the stencil in position. When the glue is dry, lift the screen and remove the tracing.

8 Lay a control sheet of printing paper on the bed and set up register stops.

9 Lower the screen, load up with colour, and take a set of control prints complete with register marks. While this is happening, the printing colour will have time to build up a good over-all adhesion between stencil and mesh.

10 Mask out the register marks on the stencil, and print the whole edition in colour NO. I.

11 Remove the screen, wash out the printing colour and remove the stencil with white (mineral) spirit or screen wash. Mop dry.

12 Wash out the spots of glue with very hot water.

13 Cut the remaining stencils, set up in register, and print in exactly the same way.

It is worth spending some time testing the properties of various kinds of papers, as not all are suitable for making knife-cut stencils. Newsprint is good, poster paper is even better. Generally speaking the paper should be thin and not overloaded with dressing. If the paper is thick, it will make a thick print. This is one of the fundamental laws of the screen process, and it needs to be emphasized. The thickness of the film of printed colour is equal to the combined thickness of mesh and stencil. If the artist wants an effect of relief or *impasto* he can get it quite easily by using a heavy duty mesh, say bolting silk 6 XX, and the thickest possible stencil, say brown wrapping paper. He could even use one of the self-adhesive protective sheets such as Fablon (UK trade name). But thick films of colour are troublesome to print, and they take a long time to dry. For all normal work the thinner the mesh and the thinner the stencil, the better.

In practice there is a limit to what the cut-paper stencil can do. It is at its best where the shapes are big and simple. Where the shapes are intricate and scattered, handling and reassembling the detached pieces becomes so difficult that even a craftsman with exceptional patience and dexterity cannot be sure of getting everything to fit. What is needed is an absolutely reliable and reasonably quick method capable of reproducing, for example, lettering down to 36 point. Early attempts to find such a method can be traced in the writings of the pioneer screen printers, but a workable solution was not found until 1930 when a patent was taken out in the United States for the first laminated stencil sheet.

Fig 14 Drawing done with a stylus on Gestescript 62½
Two men and three rockets by Felix Nelson, age four

The descendants of this original invention are in use today in every screen printing studio. Several versions are available through the specialist suppliers, but the laminated sheets sold under the trade name Stenplex (UK) or Nufilm or Profilm (US) can be taken as very good examples. Each sheet is composed of two layers bonded together by a temporary adhesive; a thin, translucent stencil sheet and a much thicker backing sheet consisting of tissue paper heavily impregnated with paraffin wax. The combined thickness is about as clear as vellum; you could read a newspaper through it. These laminated sheets should be stored flat, in a cool dry place, preferably between a couple of pieces of hardboard.

To cut a stencil, first lay the master drawing on a sheet of hardboard or, better still, on a glass-topped tracing table. Cut a piece of the laminated sheet larger than the picture space by at least $1\frac{1}{2}$ in. on all four sides. Lay the laminated sheet on the master drawing, stencil side up, and fix in place with tape. Sharpen up the stencil knife, and cut round the areas that are to print, cutting through the stencil sheet but not through the backing sheet. Lift out and remove each piece as it is cut. While you are working rest the hands on a scrap of white cardboard and avoid touching the stencil.

The screen must be properly prepared to receive the stencil. Broadly speaking, this means that the mesh must be as tight as a drum, free of grease, and dry; but detailed preparation varies slightly with the different fibres.

Cotton and silk
Sponge on both sides for about five minutes with hot water containing a liquid detergent. Rinse thoroughly with cold running water. Dry. This is standard treatment, and it applies to newly covered screens as well as to screens that have been used.

Polyamide and polyester
These filaments are too smooth to hold a stencil, and something has to be done to roughen them artificially. The manufacturer's advice should be sought, but the following method is common workshop practice. Sponge front and back for ten minutes with a 4% solution of caustic soda, using a long-handled mop, and taking care not to get a splash in the eye. Rinse thoroughly with cold running water. Then, using a damp cloth, rub the mesh front and back with a household scouring powder. Rinse thoroughly with cold running water. Dry. This treatment applies only to newly covered screens. For every time after the first, routine de-greasing consists of sponging with hot water and detergent, rinsing with cold running water, and drying.

Laminated sheets come already coated on the upper surface with a thin film of adhesive for sticking the stencil to the screen. Two kinds of adhesive are used, and the choice of one or the other for any particular job would depend on the printing colour to be used and on the mesh material in the screen. The sheets are dyed to a colour code to indicate the different adhesive coatings, thus: Amber – plasticized shellac; Blue or Green – water-soluble glues. The technique of cutting the stencil is the same in each case, but the subsequent treatment varies according to the requirements of the different adhesives.

Amber film
Shellac melts when heated and solidifies again when cool. It forms a cement which is resistant to most kinds of paint thinners, but not to cellulose. Fixing to the screen is done by means of a thermostatically controlled electric iron. Lay the stencil, shellac side up, on a sheet of hardboard, and lower the screen into contact. Cover the inside of the screen with

several thicknesses of newspaper, set the iron at 'silk' heat, and iron with light pressure until the shellac can be seen melting up into the mesh. Do not continue a minute longer than necessary, or the two layers of laminated sheet may stick together. Turn the screen over and, starting cautiously at one corner, peel off the backing sheet. When the backing sheet is safely off, lower the screen on a fresh sheet of newspaper, lay more newspaper inside, and iron once again, this time with increased pressure until the stencil is well stuck all over.

Amber film will stick without difficulty to cotton and silk. It can be made to stick to polyester multifil, although the working temperature comes dangerously near to 260°C, the melting point of this fibre.

To remove Amber film at the end of a printing run:

1 With the appropriate solvent, get rid of every trace of the printing colour. Mop dry.
2 Lay the screen on a flat surface, flood the inside with methylated spirit (alcohol), cover with a sheet of newspaper and leave for fifteen minutes.
3 By the end of this time, the methylated spirit will have dissolved the shellac coating. Lift the screen and strip off the film.
4 With a couple of cotton swabs soaked in methylated spirit, remove every trace of dilute shellac from the mesh. It is most important to do this thoroughly before the screen is taken to be de-greased, because water and dilute shellac combine to form a white solid which nothing will dissolve.

Blue film and Green film

When cellulose printing colours began to come on the market, the makers of laminated stencil sheets had to find an adhesive coating that would not be dissolved by the cellulose solvent. Blue film and Green film are the answer. Blue film was introduced in the days of cotton and silk, Green film was formulated to give better adhesion on the man-made fibres, but it also adheres well to cotton and silk. In both cases the adhesive is soluble in water.

To fix Blue film to the screen, lay the stencil face up on a sheet of hardboard and lower the screen into contact. Dip a soft rag into cold water, squeeze it as dry as possible by hand, and rub the inside of the mesh briskly over an area of about 6 in. square. Lay a sheet of clean paper over the area just damped, and iron quickly and lightly. The combination of moisture and heat will draw the glue up into the mesh. Always squeeze the rag as dry as possible: it must never be wet. Continue in the same way, square by square, until the whole area is fixed. Then turn the screen over and, beginning cautiously at one corner, peel off the backing sheet.

To fix Green film to the screen, the following materials will be required: a sheet of $\frac{1}{2}$ in. blockboard or plywood cut to a size 1 in. smaller all the way round than the inside dimensions of the screen frame; four heavy weights, say 1 lb tins of paint; electric fan or hair dryer; scrap of clean cotton cloth; cup containing a mixture of three parts of methylated spirit (alcohol) to one part of cold water. Lay the Green film on the blockboard, stencil side up. Lower the screen into contact. Make sure that the frame is not resting on the blockboard at any point. Place the weights on the four corners of the frame. Set the fan to blow across the mesh. Dip the cloth in the methylated spirit/water mixture, and squeeze it nearly dry. Then with brisk strokes damp the inside of the mesh. The art is to begin at one edge and work forward methodically from there, laying the strokes against each other like the scales of a fish. As far as possible avoid going twice over the same place, and avoid wetting any large open areas in the stencil. A strong green colour indicates that the glue has been drawn up into the mesh. Keep the fan running until the glue has dried, then switch off, take away the four weights, turn the screen over, and peel off the backing sheet.

Both Blue film and Green film are removed very easily at the end of the printing run. First clean the screen with white (mineral) spirit or screen wash to get rid of every trace of the printing colour. Mop dry. Then hose the inside of the mesh with plenty of hot water to dissolve the glue. After a few minutes the stencil will come away without difficulty, but there will still be a residue of dilute glue clinging to the mesh. This must be cleared by sponging or scrubbing the screen inside and out with hot water and detergent. Finish with a vigorous cold water rinse, and leave to dry.

10 Stencil making: serigraphic methods

In the 1920s and 1930s the silk screen process was taken up energetically by a group of young painters in the United States. They worked direct on the silk, just as the French Post-Impressionists had worked on the lithographic stone; they did their own printing, and they exhibited their prints in fine art galleries in New York and elsewhere. These were the first artists to take the medium seriously, and to claim for it a position alongside lithography.

Prints done in this manner were christened serigraphs, from the Greek, *sericos*, silk: *-graphos*, -writing. (Similarly, *lithos*, stone: *-graphos*, -writing.) The name was coined by Carl Zigrosser, Curator of Prints at Philadelphia Museum of Art, and he used it first on the occasion of an exhibition of silk screen prints at the Weyhe Gallery in New York City. This is what he said: 'A serigraph, or original silk screen print, is one which the artist made after his own design, and for which the artist himself executed the component colour stencils. All this is implied in the word *original* as applied to the Silk Screen Process, and therefore rules out any use of the term to define reproductive silk screen prints, which are copied or translated into the medium by someone other than the artist furnishing the design.'

The early serigraphic artists understood and made use of knife-cut stencils, but they were technical innovators as well. Grainy qualities intrigued them. They exploited the use of freehand brushwork and crayon drawing, they invented textures that would give an illusion of tonal gradation and depth in space. In their work they showed, for the first time, how the craft might escape from the flatness of the cut-paper style.

It will have been noticed that Zigrosser was careful not to make specific reference to any particular technique. For instance, he did not exclude the knife-cut stencil. The definition is not concerned with techniques; it is concerned with the artist becoming involved in the craft. What about photographic stencils? If they are made by the artist himself, as they often are today, there is no reason, in the terms of the definition, why they should not be considered as serigraphs. And yet this seems to be stretching the meaning of the word. Why should this be? The explanation, surely, is that serigraphy has come to be identified with the work of the pioneers and, in particular, with the freehand brush and crayon methods that they invented. This chapter is concerned with those methods.

The materials and equipment are simple. Apart from the screen itself, the only things needed are glue, varnish, liquid litho ink, wax crayons, French chalk, a selection of hog hair and sable paint brushes, and a coating trough or scraper.

The Mesh

Serigraphic work involves a large amount of screen washing, and this is a tedious and difficult job with a silk or cotton mesh. It is far better to use nylon or polyester monofilament. A good general purpose gauge is 43(10)T, with a mesh count of 109 threads to the inch. A finer mesh, say 68(20)T, with 175 threads to the inch will give finer detail.

A fine mesh will also help to minimize a trouble known as the stepped, or saw-edged, profile. This is an annoying feature common to all classes of work where a liquid filler is applied direct to the screen by brush or scraper. What happens is that the liquid wraps itself round the threads and fills the apertures in the mesh square by square. A square is either filled or it is not filled. If the artist attempts to paint a diagonal line or a curve, what he will get will be a paraphrase of his stroke correct to the nearest whole square. Clearly, the finer the mesh, the more faithful the paraphrase.

Printing colours

Any type of printing colour can be used in serigraphy, with one proviso: the solvent in the printing colour must not dissolve the screen filler. For example, fish glue (isenglass) is an excellent liquid filler; it is unaffected by colours based on oil or cellulose, and will stand up to thousands of prints. But colours based on water will soften and dissolve it in a very short time. The whole stencil making programme must be planned with this in mind.

Liquid fillers

Fish glue (isenglass) has been used as a liquid filler from the earliest days of the craft, and it still has no equal. The best kind of fish glue for the screen printer is photo-engraving glue. This remains liquid at room temperature, and can be used straight from the jar, or reduced with warm water as you wish. It gives a perfect coating. Gum arabic can be used at room temperature, and so can gouache or tempera colours. Animal glues and dextrins have to be warmed. All these fillers can be removed from the screen with hot water.

Practically any kind of brushing varnish can be used as a filler to stand up to water-based printing colours. Polyurethane varnish is excellent. Orange shellac, sometimes sold as French polish or Patent Knotting, is unaffected by both oil and water colour: it is soluble in methylated spirit. The brittleness of shellac can be overcome by adding a tablespoon of castor oil to one pint of dissolved flakes, and stirring well. All these varnishes and lacquers should be regarded as permanent fillers; it is almost impossible to get them out of the screen at the end of the run. Use them on an expendable cotton mesh for a short run, on a valuable mesh for textile printing.

Liquid litho ink is an oil-in-water emulsion, soluble in warm water while still wet, in white (mineral) spirit or turpentine when dry. It is used as a screen filler by itself, or as part of the so-called glue and tusche method. The word *tusche* is confusing because it stands for two quite different things, Indian ink and liquid litho ink. *Tusche* is the ordinary German word for Indian ink, but Indian ink cannot be used as a screen filler. The tusche used in serigraphy is liquid litho ink. (Tusche also comes in dry stick or pencil form.)

Dry fillers

By far the most important dry filler is wax crayon. Almost any kind will do, provided it can be removed from the screen at a later stage by a chemical solvent such as white (mineral) spirit or solvent naptha. The soft grades of litho crayon (NOS. 1 & 2) give good results, and so do the thick wax crayons used for taking rubbings of monumental brasses. Wax crayon

Fig 15 Serigraphic print, detail of print by the glue and tusche method, cotton organdie screen, 96 threads to the inch. Photomicrograph by Gene Cox

is used in the glue and tusche method in the same way as liquid litho ink. It can also be used by itself as a short-term filler when printing with water-based colours.

The only other interesting dry filler is French chalk. This can be used with either oil or water-based printing colour, and will give a grainy texture not unlike an aquatint ground. The effect is short-lived, because the printing colour is inclined to work its way gradually into the filler. The first few prints – perhaps a dozen with water colour, more with oil – will have a bright speckly quality; after this there will be a steady deterioration.

Method

Prepare a master drawing complete with register marks, tape it to the top of the work table, and lower the screen into contact. With a ball point or fountain pen, trace the image on to the inside of the mesh. It is safest for beginners to trace up every detail, but with experience and confidence it is usually found that a skeleton tracing is sufficient. Stencil making is potentially a messy process; drops and splashes of liquid filler and solvent occur as natural by-products, and in the interest of cleanliness the whole of this work should be done at a separate table, not on the printing bed.

A few of the most useful serigraphic methods are described below.

1 DIRECT PAINTING

Prop up the screen so that the mesh is lifted clear of the table, and fill in the negative areas by freehand brushwork. Or turn the screen over and apply the filler to the underside of the mesh; it comes to the same thing.

2 CRAYON WORK

Lower the screen into contact with a hard flat grainy surface, such as sandpaper, and rub wax crayon into the mesh, using considerable pressure. Textured surfaces such as perforated zinc and wood grain can be used in place of sandpaper. The waxed areas will come out as white in the print; in other words they are negative in the screen.

3 GLUE AND TUSCHE

This method is the serigraphic artists' gift to the silk screen process. Like lithography, it is based on the natural antipathy between oil and water. The artist draws direct on the screen, just as the lithographer draws on the stone. A positive area drawn on the screen becomes a positive area in the print. This result is arrived at in three stages, thus:

i Working on the inside of the screen, fill the positive parts of the design with litho crayon or liquid litho ink (tusche). Later on, these areas will be cleared and they will become the openings through which the printing colour will pass.

ii Set the screen up vertically and, with a coating trough or scraper, coat the inside of the mesh with a film of fish glue (isenglass). Turn the screen over, coated side down, so that the glue will not drain through to the underside of the mesh, and leave to dry. When it is dry hold the screen up to the window and look for pinholes of light, indicating that the coating is not thick enough. If necessary apply a second coat on top of the first. Do *not* coat both sides of the mesh.

iii When the glue is thoroughly dry, wash out the crayon and tusche with white (mineral) spirit or solvent naptha. The best way to do this is to lay the screen in a shallow tray, flood the mesh with the solvent, and leave for fifteen minutes. At the end of this time rub the mesh front and back with pads of cotton rag soaked in the solvent; stubborn patches can be scrubbed carefully with an old tooth brush. Continue until all the crayon and tusche areas are clear.

4 FRENCH CHALK

Make a sprinkler by knocking a large number of small holes in the lid of a tin. Lay a sheet of clean grey paper on the work bench, and cover it with a fine sprinkling of French chalk. Lower the screen gently into contact, and pour a pool of printing colour into the well at one end of the mesh. Pull the colour across with one stroke of the squeegee, and lift the screen. The French chalk will be seen clinging to the underside of the mesh, held there by the printing colour. Proceed without delay to print the edition.

This simple effect can be used by itself whenever a speckled ground is needed, or it can be added at any time to any other kind of stencil. The sprinkling of French chalk on the grey paper can be manipulated to a limited extent. One way is to drag a comb through the deposit, making parallel tracks. Other ways are by embossing, by blowing, by tapping the sheet, and by the use of temporary masks. If the result is not what was wanted, the chalk can be wiped off the screen with a rag soaked in the thinners used for removing the printing colour.

11 Stencil making: photographic methods

The older printing processes had been using photography as far back as the middle of the nineteenth century. On 29 October 1852, William Henry Fox Talbot had patented his method for making a photographic etching on a steel plate. In the following year, MM. Lemercier, Lerebours, Barreswil and Davanne had published a portfolio of prints entitled *Lithophotographie; ou, Impressions obtenues sur pierre à l'aide de la photographie*. Thus it is not surprising that the early screen printers should have found themselves speculating on the possibility of bringing photography into their craft.

The first attempts were based, not unnaturally, on Fox Talbot's original work. He had discovered that when a solution of potassium bichromate and gelatine are mixed together, the resulting complex is sensitive to light. If exposed to light it becomes insoluble in water; if protected from the light it remains soluble. From this one reaction two successful techniques have been developed, the Direct and the Indirect. In the first the mesh itself is coated with the light-sensitive gelatine/bichromate mixture; in the second a film of gelatine is sensitized, exposed and developed away from the screen, and transferred to the mesh only at the end of the process. Both methods are in everyday use in screen printing studios.

The direct method

A stencil made by the direct method is immensely tough and hard-wearing; it will not break down in the middle of a long run. It is the best kind of stencil for printing textiles and wallpaper.

The process needs a darkroom, or at least an effective arrangement of black curtains over the windows, and an orange safe light to work by. Coating the screen is a slow job, but this can be speeded up if there is a drying cupboard fitted with horizontal racks. When the coating has been hardened by the action of light it is difficult, if not impossible, to get it out of the mesh. Prints from a direct-coated screen used to be bedevilled by the stepped or saw-edged profile, but with modern materials this trouble has been practically eliminated.

THREE RECIPES FOR SENSITIZED COATINGS
The ingredients for the first can be bought in any small town.

Method
Dissolve 10 oz gelatine in 100 fluid oz boiling water. Dissolve 1 oz potassium bichromate in 60 fluid oz hot water. Stir the two solutions together and strain. This mixture must be applied hot, because animal gelatine solidifies as it cools.

Fish glue (isenglass) makes an excellent photo-sensitive coating, and it can be used at ordinary room temperature.

RECIPE USING NORLAND PHOTOENGRAVING GLUE
Materials

Norland Photoengraving Glue	7 fluid oz
potassium bichromate	1 oz
water	17 fluid oz

Method
Dissolve the bichromate in the water and then mix with the glue. Filter through cotton and it is ready to use. The amount of water can be varied to make it heavier or thinner. Distilled water or deionized water is preferable, but good tap water can be used.

An emulsion of polyvinyl alcohol (PVA) when mixed with a solution of ammonium bichromate reacts to light in much the same way as a gelatine/bichromate mixture. Applied to the screen as a direct coating, dried and exposed to the light, it will harden to an insoluble leathery film. This film, though very tenacious, is more or less independent of the structure of the mesh; it can follow any diagonal or curve in the artist's original drawing without reducing it to zig-zags. Alcoset is an excellent example of a modern PVA photo-stencil emulsion. (Alcoset is a UK trade name. Similar materials are manufactured by many different companies in the US.)

RECIPE USING ALCOSET
Materials

ammonium bichromate	16 oz
warm water	7 pints
Alcoset	

Method

Make a stock solution by dissolving the ammonium bichromate in the warm water. When required for use mix 1 part stock solution with 5 parts Alcoset. After mixing, leave for two or three hours to allow time for air bubbles to escape. Once mixed with the sensitizing solution Alcoset is light sensitive. Keep it in a closed dark glass container, away from extremes of heat and cold.

Before the screen is coated, the mesh must be thoroughly cleaned, de-greased, rinsed and dried. The coating can be put on by brush, scraper or coating trough: the coating trough gives by far the best results. Begin by coating the mesh on the inside, and lay the screen, coated side down, in a warm, dark, dust-free place to dry. The temperature must not exceed 105°F (40°C). When the first coat is perfectly dry apply a second coat, this time to the underside of the mesh. Lay the screen coated side up to dry. Two coats should be enough to fill the mesh, so that when the screen is held up to the safe light no pinholes can be seen. If more coats are needed these should all be applied to the underside of the mesh. When the last coat is dry the screen is ready to receive the exposure, and the sooner this can be done the better.

Making a photographic stencil is really a form of contact printing. A transparent positive is held in contact with the sensitized coating, a powerful lamp is set up at a measured distance from it and switched on for a measured period of time. During the exposure the coating becomes insoluble except where it is covered by the opaque parts of the positive. After the exposure the screen is rinsed in running water until all the soluble parts of the coating have been washed away. Thus a black image on the original transparent positive becomes at the end of the process an open area in the stencil. And, as with all other kinds of stencils, the mesh is either filled or it is not filled: the process cannot reproduce gradations.

The transparent positive can be drawn on tracing paper, but this is inclined to wrinkle and go out of shape. It is better to use one of the clear acetate tracing films like Astrafoil or Kodatrace (in the US Dull Mat, Trace-o-Line, or Trace-o-Mat). The positive image should be drawn in opaque ink, paint, or black crayon. Pelikan Drawing Ink TT is a good example of an opaque ink especially made for this work. The original need not be strictly a drawing; it could be a collage of any flat, opaque material glued to the transparent sheet. Things like ferns, feathers, string, lace, and perforated metal foil are all worth trying. Instant lettering, and the whole range of symbols and mechanical tints manufactured by Letraset Ltd, can be reproduced on the screen by this process. And so can high-contrast photo-positives printed on Kodalith Films.

The easiest way to set up the exposure is to hang the lamp from the ceiling and lay the screen on a flat working surface beneath it. The same arrangement works equally well with the direct and the indirect photographic methods, and the same apparatus can be used for both.

A direct coated screen is normally exposed with its underside facing the source of light. Make a block with a hard flat top half an inch smaller all round than the inside dimensions of the screen, and with sides slightly deeper than the sides of the screen frame. Cut a piece of $\frac{1}{4}$ in. foam sheeting to cover the top of the block. Arrange the screen over the block with the inside of the mesh resting on the foam sheeting. Lay the transparent positive *face down* on the underside of the mesh and fix in place with tape.

The secret of success in all these photographic processes is perfect contact between transparent positive and sensitized coating. This is achieved by applying some form of pressure. The most primitive way is to cover the transparent positive with a sheet of $\frac{1}{4}$ in. plate glass, and put a heavy weight on each corner. This is good enough for first attempts, and will give satisfactory results, provided the drawing contains no fine detail. An arrangement of pressure bars operated by wing nuts, as in a photographer's contact printing frame, will reproduce fine lines and small type, provided the transparent positive is free of wrinkles. But for best results there is nothing to equal a vacuum frame.

The Copysac made by Screen Process Supplies Ltd is a very good example of a simple vacuum frame. (A US equivalent is the Nu-Arc photo contact table.) The Copysac consists of a large transparent plastic bag open at one end. A length of pressure tubing leads from an outlet at the far end of the bag to a stainless steel water jet vacuum pump. The coated screen, supported on its block and with the transparent positive taped in position, is slipped into the bag. The mouth of the bag is folded over twice and closed with a row of large bull-dog clips (clamps). The pump is turned on. As the air is withdrawn the bag becomes flattened by the pressure of the normal atmosphere outside. The pump is left running to maintain the vacuum throughout the exposure period.

The cheapest type of lamp, and the simplest to install, is a photographers' NO. 2 Photoflood light bulb. This can be plugged into an ordinary socket and run straight off the mains supply. A mercury vapour lamp such as Philips 125 w MBR/U Repro lamp gives a far better light and has a much longer life. This lamp has to be run in conjunction with a ballast and capacitor. Any capable electrician can rig up this circuit for himself, or the whole assembly can be bought ready made from the specialist suppliers.

It can be taken as a working rule that a lamp will illuminate a circular area with a diameter equal to the perpendicular distance between the lamp and the working surface. In other words if the transparent positive is 18 in. across the lamp should be set no higher than 18 in. above it. It is strongly recommended that this height should be worked out from the dimensions of the standard screen and that once it has been set up the lamp should not be moved.

There is no simple rule for calculating the time of the exposure, because there are too many variable factors in the situation: the composition and thickness of the sensitized coating, the opacity of the positive, the strength of the lamp, and so on. But as a very rough guide, a NO. 2 Photoflood lamp set at 18 in. will need about eighteen minutes, a mercury vapour lamp at the same distance will need about five minutes. The exact time can only be found by a controlled test.

Take a sample positive (say a sheet of Instant lettering), mark it out in parallel bands, fix it to a coated screen in the usual way, and cover with a sheet of card. Switch on the light and, at intervals of two minutes, pull the card back to the next mark. When the screen is developed, there will be no difficulty in deciding which of the bands has been correctly exposed; the insoluble parts will be thick, the soluble parts will be clear, and all the edges will be sharp. The findings of this test can be relied on to apply to all subsequent exposures, so long as the conditions are not varied.

After the exposure, the transparent positive should be retrieved and put away in a safe place. The screen is developed by rinsing with cold water for two minutes, then with water at 100°F (37°C) until all the soluble parts have been dissolved and washed out of the mesh. It is now safe, for the first time, to pull back the curtains or switch on full normal lighting in the room. Examine the mesh very carefully to make sure that no scum is left in the open parts of the design. Wipe over with a clean chamois leather, and leave in a horizontal position until dry.

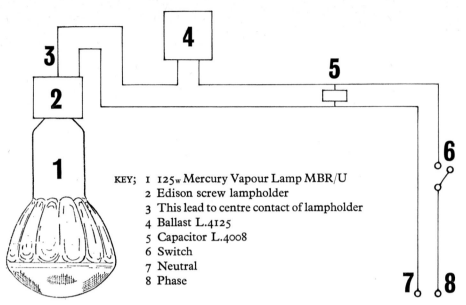

KEY; 1 125w Mercury Vapour Lamp MBR/U
2 Edison screw lampholder
3 This lead to centre contact of lampholder
4 Ballast L.4125
5 Capacitor L.4008
6 Switch
7 Neutral
8 Phase

Fig 16 Mercury vapour lamp installation. Circuit diagram by courtesy of Philips Electrical Ltd

This is the end of the photographic process, but textile printers sometimes go on from here and reinforce the stencil by varnishing. This is the method:

Lay the screen down in the printing position, but propped up on a vacant frame so that the mesh is lifted clear of the table. With a 2 in. brush apply a coat of polyurethane varnish all over the inside of the mesh. Turn the screen over immediately, and wipe the underside of the mesh vigorously with a pad of cotton rag just slightly damp with white (mineral) spirit. Change to a fresh piece of rag as often as necessary, and continue without stopping until all the varnish has been drawn up out of the open parts of the design. Leave the screen where it is until the varnish is dry.

Varnishing adds an extra protective layer to the stencil, and leaves it with a smooth, polished surface. During printing the colour flows more freely and is less likely to clog. Washing the screen takes half the time.

The indirect method

The technique of indirect photo-stencil making consists, essentially, in the manipulation of a thin film of photographic gelatine. As this film is no thicker than 0·001 in. (0·025 mm), it can only be handled in the form of a coating adhering to the surface of a temporary support. Two supports are needed, and during the process the gelatine is transferred from one to the other. Finally, after exposure and development, the finished stencil is transferred from the second temporary support to the mesh.

This double transfer method was first used in the early days of photographic printing, long before the arrival of the silk screen process: it was invented by Joseph Wilson Swan, and patented by him on 29 February 1864. The method ran like this:

1 Coat a sheet of paper with gelatine.
2 Sensitize in a solution of potassium bichromate.
3 Expose to light.
4 Transfer to an India rubber temporary support.
5 Develop in warm water.
6 Peel off the paper support.
7 Transfer the gelatine to the final support, and leave to dry.

76

8 Remove the India rubber.

The modern screen printer's technique is descended in a direct line from this invention.

In January 1868, the rights of Swan's patent were acquired by the Autotype Printing and Publishing Company, and shortly after the first world war this firm introduced the first of their gelatine coated papers to the screen printing trade. From that day onwards new and improved versions of the original process have appeared on the market, and no doubt will continue to appear. The version to be described in this chapter was introduced in about 1945: it is probably the most widely used photo-stencil process in professional screen printing studios and in art schools in Great Britain today.

The process has several advantages:

1 A dark room is not needed.

2 The whole operation takes less than half an hour.

3 The stencil is completely independent of the structure of the mesh, and will follow any diagonal or curve in the artist's original without reducing it to zig-zags.

4 A well-made stencil will give thousands of prints so long as oil or cellulose printing colour is used.

5 At the end of the run the stencil can be washed out of the mesh without difficulty, leaving the screen clear for another job.

This is a wet printing process: once the coated paper has been dipped in the sensitizing solution, there must be no stopping until the stencil is safely on the screen. For this reason everything must be laid out ready and checked carefully before work starts.

The furniture and equipment, the lamp installation and contact printing frame are the same as would be used in the direct photo-stencil process. In addition a large photographic dish will be needed, a thermometer, a small squeegee, a supply of clean cotton rags, and some old newspaper. The special materials are:

1 Autotype coated paper 1045/2 or Universal Red. This comes in the form of a continuous roll: it can be stored indefinitely provided the atmosphere is neither excessively dry nor excessively damp.

2 The temporary support. This is a clear transparent plastic sheet manufactured in the form of a continuous roll with a thickness of 0·002 in. (0·05 mm). Good examples are Astrafoil and Extrafoil (in the US Trace-o-Line, Trace-o-Mat or Dull Mat).

In addition a clear wax polish will be needed, and a 2% solution of potassium bichromate.

A screen newly covered with a nylon or polyester mesh must be swabbed in a 4% solution of caustic soda, rubbed gently with a household abrasive, and rinsed very thoroughly in running water. An old screen must be thoroughly cleaned, de-greased and rinsed.

Cut a piece of Autotype coated paper 1 in. larger all round than the image on the master drawing. Cut a piece of the temporary support 1 in. larger all round than the Autotype paper. Wax one side of the temporary support, and polish until the thinnest possible film of wax is left.

Make up a 2% solution of potassium bichromate at 60°–65°F (15°–18°C), and strain it into the photographic dish. Immerse the temporary support, waxed side up, in the solution. Immerse the Autotype paper, coated side up, in the solution on top of the temporary support. Leave for two minutes.

Lift the Autotype paper by two corners and turn it over, coated side down. Pick up the Autotype paper and temporary support together, face to face, and hold up by the corners to drain. Lay the sandwich on the white Formica working surface, with the Autotype paper on top, the temporary support beneath. Press the two sheets together, using the little squeegee at an angle of about 45°, and taking care to drive out any trapped air bubbles. Mop off the surplus bichromate solution and then turn the sandwich over, temporary support side up, on to a sheet of newspaper. With a dry cloth, clean and polish the surface of the temporary support.

Arrange the transparent positive *face down* in the centre of the temporary support, and fix the corners with tape. Insert in the contact frame and expose under the lamp. The general advice on distance and exposure given in the section on direct photo-stencils applies equally well to indirect stencils. When setting up a new installation it is essential to begin with a methodical pilot test.

While the exposure is in process, there are two things to be done:

1 Wash the bichromate solution off the hands – it is a poison.
2 Prepare the photographic dish with about one inch of water at 100°–110°F (38°–43°C). This temperature must be measured with a thermometer, it must not be guessed.

After the exposure, retrieve the transparent positive and put it away in a safe place. Immerse the exposed sandwich, paper side up, in the bath of warm water.

The gelatine coating on Autotype papers is impregnated with a dye so that, when the process has reached this stage, the printer can see what is happening. A few moments after the sandwich has been lowered into the warm water, the dye will be seen oozing out from the edges. This is a sign that the soluble parts of the gelatine are beginning to dissolve. Give it another minute and then with one hand hold down the edge of the temporary support and with the other carefully peel off the backing paper and throw it away. It will now be seen that during the exposure the gelatine film has transferred itself to the surface of the temporary support.

Lift the temporary support by the two far corners and lay it on an inclined sheet of plate glass or white Formica. Rinse the gelatine film with water at 100°–110°F, using a sprinkler or watering can with a fine rose. Continue until all the open parts of the stencil are showing perfectly clear and colourless. Then chill the gelatine by rinsing it with cold water for about a minute.

Take a piece of hardboard smaller than the inside dimensions of the screen frame but larger than the temporary support, and cover the top with newspaper. Lay the temporary support, gelatine side up, on the newspaper. Lower the screen on to the surface of the gelatine; it must go straight down in the right place the first time. Place heavy weights on the four corners of the screen frame.

The moisture in the gelatine must now be drawn up into the mesh. Spread a sheet of

Fig 17 Indirect photo-stencil from a high contrast transparent positive

clean blotting paper or newspaper on the inside of the mesh, and press it very gently with the palms of the hands or with a soft composition roller. Change the paper for a dry piece, and continue until all the excess moisture has been absorbed. Leave the stencil to dry out naturally, or accelerate the drying with a warm air blower. This treatment must not be continued for too long or the gelatine may curl away from the mesh.

When the gelatine is really dry remove the weights, turn the screen over, and peel off the temporary support. The waxing of the temporary support was designed to make this a clean and easy separation. If there is any difficulty it means that the gelatine is not yet dry enough, and drying must be continued a little longer. When the temporary support is safely off, it can be cleaned up and used again and again.

An indirect photo-stencil is normally used by printers working with oil or cellulose colour. It will not stand up to an industrial run with water-based textile printing colours. However, if reinforced on the inside with polyurethane varnish it will certainly last long enough for the amateur to print a dress length.

12 Printing colours

In this chapter the word colour is used, somewhat loosely, to describe all those liquids that can be printed through the screen. Understood in this way the term covers not only printing inks but varnishes, glues, and thickened textile dyes. The full list of screen colours used in industry would include a hundred and one special formulations, such as the resists and frits used in the printing of electronic circuitry, glass and ceramics. There may be no chemical relationship between these substances, but where they must all agree, as far as the printer is concerned, is in their working properties or physical characteristics.

The most critical of these, and yet the most elusive is the one that printers have in mind when they talk about their colour having the correct 'flow'. The squeegee must be able to travel easily, as if lubricated by the colour. There must be no frothing. When the screen is raised after making a print, the minute dots of colour forced through the mesh must run together immediately and unite to form a continuous film of colour, and yet there must be no tendency for the edge of the pattern to spread. The colour must not dry in the mesh, and yet the prints should dry quickly.

Printing colour should also be durable. It should be compatible with the surface to which it is applied; it should not crack, blister, or rub off. It should be fast to light and to the effects of atmospheric pollution.

This book is not concerned with the industrial applications of screen printing; it is concerned with the individual artist who wants to work out his own ideas as prints. The best way to learn the craft is by printing on paper. Once the basic skills have been acquired, it is only a short step to printing on sheet metal, plastic or glass. Any artist who wants to print on an out-of-the-ordinary material has only to write to the specialist suppliers for advice on a suitable printing colour; they will certainly have what he needs.

For practical purposes, screen printing colours can be divided into those that are based on water, and those that are not. This is an important distinction. Water-based colours are considerably cheaper to buy than oil or cellulose colours, and they are very much cheaper to use. The simple reason for this is that water costs less than chemical solvents. In a studio where oil or cellulose colours are used, the amount spent in a year on thinners and solvents may equal, if not exceed, the cost of the colours themselves. When working with water-based colours, the type of stencil has to be chosen with care: for example, stencils cut from Amber film will last for hundreds of prints, but Blue film will collapse in a very short time. Water-based colours are thin and almost transparent; they have a freshness that no other kind of colour can imitate. The nearest equivalent is the colour used by Hokusai.

Water-based colours

By far the cheapest screen printing colour is the simple two-part mix: a watery paste tinted with a textile dye. Make the paste first, using any of these recipes:*

STARCH PASTE

Materials
20 parts laundry starch or rice flour
200 parts cold water
5–10 parts vegetable oil
all parts by weight.

Method
Work the starch to a smooth creamy paste with a little of the water. Add the remainder of the water, little by little, and then the oil, stirring all the time. Boil gently and stir continuously until the starch thickens, and for a minute afterwards. Turn off the heat, remove the pan, and stir the starch as it cools: this part of the work is most important, but usually neglected.

SODIUM ALGINATE PASTE
Sodium alginate is manufactured from seaweed, and sold as a straw-coloured powder under the trade name Manutex (UK) or Keltex (USA).

Recipe using Manutex
Materials
12·5 grams sodium hexametaphosphate (Calgon)
20 grams Manutex R.S.
1 litre cold water.

Method
1 Dissolve the Calgon in a little of the water which, for this purpose, may be warmed if necessary to about 60°C (140°F).
2 Add the remainder of the cold water
3 Stir the Calgon solution briskly, and pour in the Manutex powder as a steady stream or drift. Continue stirring until the Manutex particles have swollen and formed a thick suspension (five to ten minutes).
4 Leave to stand for a further twenty minutes, during which time the paste will assume a clear, uniform, glassy texture.
5 Give a final short stir just before use.

Recipe using Keltex
To make a 5% stock paste (128 oz):

Materials
102 oz cold water

* In the US paints can be purchased ready made and used straight from the can. The average screen printer, whether professional or amateur, can purchase any colour he may require in an art supply store.

0·62 cc preservative (Dowicide A)
0·41 cc ammonia 28%
127 grams Improved Keltex S.

Method
1 Add preservative and ammonia to water.
2 Under high-speed agitation, quickly sprinkle Keltex into solution.
3 After thirty minutes of mixing the paste is ready for use.

A paste very similar to the two foregoing can be made by stirring 4 level teaspoons of Polycell paperhanging powder into one pint of cold water, leaving for fifteen minutes, and then giving a final stir.

These alginate pastes are all made with cold water, and they must not be boiled. When made up they will keep in good condition in a covered jar for several weeks. If, during printing, there should be any tendency for the paste to set in the mesh, this can be prevented by stirring in 2 drops (not more) of glycerine to every cupful of mix.

THE DYE
Prepare a concentrated solution of any of the dyes sold in small packages for home dyeing, thus:
Measure one level teaspoon of dye powder into a clean cup. Add a few drops of cold water. With the back of a stainless steel spoon, grind the dye against the side of the cup until it attains the consistency of smooth cream. Now add boiling water, drop by drop, until the cream becomes a solution, or at least a colloidal suspension. Leave to cool.

Add the dye solution, a drop at a time, to the watery paste, until the desired saturation has been reached. These dye solutions are very strong, and it is easy to add too much. The best way is to proceed cautiously, making frequent tests of the colour on a sheet of white paper.

A favourite trick of the Japanese masters was to run a band of indigo across the top of the print, fading out the lower edge to nothing, as if mists were rising on the morning of a fine day. This effect can be reproduced exactly in the screen. Pour a supply of clear watery paste into the well at one end of the screen, running it right across from side to side except for a small space in one corner. Pour a small pool of indigo coloured paste into this corner. Make a print. As the squeegee travels across the mesh, the indigo will blend with the un-coloured paste in a band of almost perfect gradation. With a bit of practice it is not difficult to recharge the screen at the end of each stroke, and so to produce an edition. The width of the graded band will vary slightly from print to print, but less than might be imagined.

These watery pastes have been discussed at some length because they are not as well known as they deserve to be. They bring screen printing within reach of the school teacher working within a tight budget; and in this context there is no reason why the same mixture should not be applied in other ways, as with a brush, or by paste combing. But, cost apart, the watery pastes have their own unique, luminous quality. The loud side of the screen process is well enough known; its quiet side is almost unexplored.

Emulsion colours
Although it would be very easy to print on textiles with any of the watery pastes just des-cribed, the simple act of printing is not sufficient to fix the colour. If the material were to be washed, the colour would run. The fixation of dyes in textile fibres is a study in itself: it lies outside the scope of the present book, but is dealt with in the author's *Fabric Printing*

by Hand. Printed dyes are normally fixed by a steam treatment, and this means buying or making a special piece of apparatus called a steamer. Another complication is that dyes are by nature selective; the dye that will dye wool may not dye cotton, and *vice versa*. With home-made equipment it is very difficult for the amateur to fix any kind of dye on the man-made fibres.

All these difficulties can be avoided by using not dyes but one of the modern pigment pastes based on an oil-in-water emulsion. These colours, originally formulated for textile printing, can be used equally well on paper. The ingredients are mixed together cold, according to the manufacturer's instructions, and the resulting paste is immediately ready for use. At the end of the printing run, screen and squeegee are rinsed in cold running water. The printed material is left to dry, and then fixed by dry heat. The heat treatment can be applied to prints on both paper and textiles. In this way the printer has the best of both worlds: while he is working he can wash up under the tap, and yet his finished product is a waterproof print. Two typical recipes follow:

RECIPE I: POLYPRINT COLOURS (UK) or ACCO-LITE (USA)

If possible, prepare the fabric by steeping it overnight in a solution of one teaspoonful of malt extract per gallon of warm water. Next morning wash the fabric, dry and iron it ready for printing.

Mix together cold:

	DEEP SHADE	MEDIUM SHADE	PALE SHADE
Polyprint colour	10	4	0·5
Polyprint binder	90	96	99·5
	100	100	100

ALL PARTS BY VOLUME

Allow each colour to dry before overprinting with the next. Leave the finished material to dry overnight before fixing. Fix by baking for 3 minutes at 280°F in an electric oven. If there is no oven, fix by ironing the back of the material with an iron set at 'cotton' heat.

RECIPE 2: PRINTEX FABRIC PRINTING COLOURS

These colours are prepared by Winsor and Newton Ltd from Tinolite colour by Geigy (UK) Ltd.

The fabric to be printed should be thoroughly washed, rinsed and dried. Prints on cotton and viscose rayon have the best fastness to washing; prints on silk, wool and synthetic materials like nylon can be hand washed, but the colours will not withstand severe abrasive washing. Fabrics which have been treated to give a permanent glaze or a crease-resist finish can be used, but the results are usually not so good as on untreated fabrics. Fastness to light is good on all materials.

Mix together cold:

	3% CONCENTRATION	5% CONCENTRATION
Printex colour	I teaspoon	I teaspoon
Printex binder	10 tablespoons	6 tablespoons

Colours can be mixed with one another to give any desired hue, whilst paler colours can be obtained by increasing the amount of binder. Opaque effects will be obtained by mixing colours with white.

White printing paste (for all purposes)

Printex white 4 teaspoons

Printex binder 5 teaspoons

Allow the printed material to dry thoroughly, and then fix by baking for 3 minutes at 300°F, or by ironing on the back with an iron set at 'cotton' heat.

Thin film inks

One of the greatest obstacles facing the pioneer screen printers was the lack of any oil-based printing colour with a satisfactory flow. The best colours available in the early 1920s were the ordinary signwriter's paints and enamels, but these were so thin that they tended to flood under the stencil. Attempts to thicken them up by leaving the lid off the tin, or by stirring in French chalk merely caused the screen to clog. These remedies may sound barbaric today, but at the time there was no other choice.

The problem of flow was not going to be solved overnight, and the first colours to be sold as screen printing inks fell a long way short of perfection. They consisted of finely ground solid pigments suspended in traditional boiled oils and varnishes. They formed a skin in the can, and constant vigilance was necessary to prevent them from doing the same in the screen. The prints were thick and leathery; they took a long time to dry, and even when dry they were easily damaged by scuffing. There is still a demand for these colours, and they are still being made.

In 1947 an entirely new and revolutionary class of colours appeared for the first time on the open market in Great Britain: this was the DH 186 range of Cellulose Screen Printing Inks developed in the laboratory of the Cellon Works at Kingston-upon-Thames. The discovery had an interesting history. One of the curious bottle-necks in factory production in wartime Britain was the job of printing labels and instructions on such articles as life rafts and buoyancy bags. The antiquated method of printing through die-cut stencils was hopelessly inadequate, and Cellon set themselves the task of formulating a quick-drying cellulose 'paste' so that the job could be done by the screen. The successful outcome of this research led directly to the DH 186 cellulose inks. In 1956 the same firm introduced a companion range of colours soluble in white (mineral) spirit. Printing inks of similar composition are now available from most of the specialist manufacturers. They are always referred to as 'thin film' inks.

In his *Handbook of Graphic Reproduction Processes* (1962) Felix Brunner gave it as his opinion that ' . . . the essential feature of silk screen prints is the thick, paste-like coating of colour'. This may have been true of the old oil colours, but it is certainly not a fair description of the thin film inks. Anyone who has visited an exhibition of screen prints done since 1957 will have seen for himself that thick, paste-like coatings of colour are not an essential feature of silk screen prints.

The thin film inks come in a range of brilliant, pure colours, all of which can be mixed together freely, in any combination, so as to produce compound shades. The colour is made too stiff to be used straight from the can; it is made like this intentionally so that the printer can do his own thinning to suit the job in hand. As a very rough guide, the colours should be reduced in the ratio – colour, 80 : white (mineral) spirit, 20. They will in fact tolerate a dilution in the ratio – colour, 60 : white (mineral) spirit, 40, but no beginner ever believes this until he has tried. Generally speaking, colour should be used as thin as it is safe to use it. An absorbent surface will take the colour in a very liquid state, a non-absorbent surface needs to have it thicker.

The colour in the stock can should never be thinned or altered in any way. The correct procedure is to take out a little on the blade of a clean palette knife, and to work it on a slab of marble or plate glass or in a small container, adding white (mineral) spirit a little at a time until the desired consistency is reached. The finished mix should be of an even consistency through and through; no lumps, no streaks of unmixed colour.

When reduced in white spirit, the thin film inks dry with a smooth, matt finish. The colours are all more or less opaque, and this means that white can be printed over black. But not all colours are as opaque as white; the degree of opacity varies from one colour to another, and the beginner should get to know the opacity of his colours by running a series of tests, printing and overprinting in every possible combination. The results of these tests should be kept for future reference. To get the maximum opacity, the colours should be used fairly thick.

But the artist may not always want his colours to be opaque; he is just as likely to want to use them sometimes as a transparent coloured glaze. Adding white spirit makes the colours more transparent, but in doing so it makes them more liquid. What is needed is a reducing medium that is both transparent and stiff. To meet this need, all manufacturers of thin film inks make a clear, colourless paste called 'transparent base'. Like the colours themselves, the base is supplied too stiff to be used straight from the can; it has to be thinned by the printer.

When making a mixture of colour and transparent base, always begin with the base. Take out a little on the blade of a clean palette knife and work it on a marble slab, adding white (mineral) spirit little by little until the desired consistency is reached. Then stir in the colour, taking care not to add too much all at once, because once it has been added it cannot be taken out again. By varying the proportions of the three ingredients, ink, transparent base and white spirit, the printer can get practically any degree he likes of thickness, thinness, opacity or transparency.

Colour matching should always be done slowly and carefully, stopping at frequent intervals to test a sample on a sheet of white paper. Always make up too much rather than too little, making due allowance for 'wetting out' the screen and taking trial proofs. It is a serious matter to run out of colour half way through an edition. If there should be any colour left over at the end, this need not be wasted, because the thin film inks do not dry up or form a skin in the can. A special shelf in the paint cupboard should be reserved for odds and ends of mixed colour: they will be used sooner or later.

The thin film inks will print on all types of paper and card, on hardboard and on wood. They can be used with all types of mesh and all types of stencil except those where wax crayon and tusche are used as direct fillers. They are very economical in use; one pint of colour will print an area of 30,000 square inches.

The thin film inks are what is called self solvent. In practice this means that the printer can safely leave the colour in the mesh during a meal break or even overnight. Before going off, sweep the colour up to one end and return as much as possible to the container. On resuming work, pour the colour back into the screen and take a few waste pulls on old newspaper. The new colour will soften up the old, and the screen will clear itself. If there should be any stubborn patches, lower the screen on to old newspaper, and rub the inside of the mesh with cotton rag made just damp with white spirit. Do not flood the screen.

In a properly ventilated workshop, drying time is about fifteen minutes for the first colour, more than that for subsequent colours. The first colour must be perfectly dry before attempting to overprint. The solvent vapour is heavier than air, and if extractor fans are being installed to assist ventilation these should be fitted at floor level.

Screen varnishes

The screen makes an excellent tool for applying a coat of clear varnish to a flat surface; the deposit is very even, and there are no brush marks. Special varnishes are made to go with all the different kinds of screen printing inks, and the suppliers will always advise on the best choice for any particular job.

As an example, a print made with thin film inks will dry with a naturally matt finish: an all-over printing of clear screen varnish will convert this to a glossy finish, and at the same time protect the print against damage by rubbing.

Another way to use varnish is to apply it to parts of the print only, exploiting the contrast between matt and glossy surfaces. To do this, a stencil can be made to take varnish just as if it were any ordinary colour. All types of stencil are suitable, including photographic stencils with fine lines and dots.

Metallic colours

'Gold' and 'Silver' screen colours can be had ready mixed from some suppliers, but it is more usual for the printer to mix his own. The recipe is very simple, there are only two ingredients:

1 Fine metallic powder, either aluminium or bronze, with names like Superior Gold, Deep Copper and Antique Bronze.

2 A special metallic medium which is made for the screen printer; but good results can be had with quick-drying signwriter's gold size.

Pour a little of the medium into a mixing can, add the metallic powder, and stir well. The right consistency can be found without much difficulty by trial and error, and the necessary adjustment made there and then. If there is too much medium, the print will be transparent; if there is too much powder, the screen will clog. Make up just enough for the day's work, because freshly made metallic colour is always more brilliant than old stock.

The metallic colours are more likely than any other kind of printing colour to cause the screen to clog. If possible, use a nylon or polyester mesh, not finer than 43(10)T. Plan the work so that the whole edition can be run off without a break. Recruit a helper to stack the wet prints. Use a squeegee with a clean, sharp blade. Between each print and the next, use the technique of flood coating described in the next chapter.

When used in conjunction with other colours in a multi-colour job, the metallic colours are normally printed last.

Gilding

There is no reason why the screen printer should not, for a special job, enjoy the luxury of working with real gold. All the materials can be bought from an old-fashioned oil and colour merchant, an art supply store or a signwriter's supplier; in fact, this is a signwriter's method.

Materials:

1 French chalk done up in a little muslin bag.

2 Gold leaf. This is sold in books containing 25 leaves. Each leaf measures about $3\frac{1}{4}$ in. square by about 1/200,000 in. thick. The easiest kind for the amateur to handle is called Transfer Gold Leaf, where the gold is supported on a temporary backing sheet of tissue paper.

3 Gold size (or mordant). The different grades of gold size are usually labelled according

to the time they take to dry – '1½ hours', '4 to 5 hours', '16 hours' and so on. The gold size can be tinted by mixing in a little red or yellow ochre oil colour.

Method
Rub French chalk all over the surface to be printed, and dust off surplus with a dry cotton cloth. Screen on the gold size, and leave until it has dried to exactly the right tacky condition to receive the gold. This is the critical moment. As Graily Hewitt said, 'To know the exact time to allow between laying and gilding, one had need to be a meteorologist, so much "depends on the weather".' Cennino Cennini, writing in the early fifteenth century, gave good advice, 'feel what you have done with the ring-finger of the right hand, that is, with the tip of the finger, and if it is only slightly tacky, then take the pincers, cut off half a leaf of fine gold, or alloyed gold, or of silver, though these two do not last, and lay it upon the mordant. Press it with cotton, and with the same finger stroke the piece of gold, putting some over the mordant where there is none. Don't do it with any other finger-tip, for this is the most sensitive and delicate of the whole hand, and take care that your hands are always clean.'

Begin at one edge, and work methodically forward, laying each leaf against the previous one, like tiles on a roof. If the state of tackiness has been correctly judged, the gold will transfer itself immediately on contact, and the tissue will come away cleanly. When the whole area has been done, cover the work with a sheet of clean paper, and rub lightly with cotton wool (absorbent cotton). Leave overnight to dry. Next day brush off the surplus gold with a piece of cotton wool (absorbent cotton).

Flocking
Perhaps the most familiar examples of flocking are the rich, velvet-textured wallpapers so often found in oriental restaurants. Flocked paper of this kind was originally introduced as a cheap alternative to cut velvet wall coverings. The first patent was that taken out by Jerome Lanyer on 1 May 1634, in which he described a 'pile' of wool and silk, held to the paper by a mixture of varnish and neat's foot oil.

The flocking powder used for making decorative papers today consists, normally, of a fine chaff of coloured rayon. The adhesive is either a straight varnish or a mixture of varnish and printing ink matched to suit the colour of the flocking powder.

Method
Screen on a generous coat of varnish. Carry the printed sheet to a cubicle in a distant corner of the room, far removed from the screen, and lay it printed side up on a clean flat table. While the varnish is still wet, shake down on to it a thick deposit of flocking powder, using a fine hair sieve or a flour dredger held about a yard above the surface of the sheet. The powder will embed itself in the wet varnish by its own weight. Leave until the varnish is dry, then shake off the surplus flocking powder and return it to the container.

Other kinds of powder, such as silver and coloured 'glitters' can be applied by exactly the same method.

13 Printing
The secret of smooth and trouble-free printing is to have everything organized, and all the materials and equipment checked before colour is put into the screen. As far as possible the

day should be planned so that the whole edition can be printed straight off without a break, because if things are going to go wrong, they will go wrong when printing is interrupted. It is very much easier to keep up a steady, rhythmical output if two people can work together as a team: the printer concentrates on printing, and the helper takes away the wet prints and hangs them up to dry. Textile and wallpaper printing on the long table is, in any case, a two-man job.

The first thing to check is the screen. If the frame is warped or the mesh slack, the printing colour is almost certain to flood under the stencil. We must hope that the craftsman has not come as far as this without looking to see that his frame is not warped. A warped frame can only be corrected by planing, and the time to do this is before putting on the mesh.

A slack mesh can lead to endless trouble in printing and, unfortunately, there is very little that can be done to put it right. It is far easier to avoid the problem altogether, by using a nylon or polyester mesh, and stretching it on a master frame. But if the mesh is found to be slack just before printing is due to begin, something has to be done. When the mesh has been fastened to the screen by the method of pinning and glueing to the outside edges of the frame but not to the face side, it is possible to do something. Cut some long narrow strips of card or well-sandpapered wood, about as thick as an ordinary ruler, and force them into the space between the mesh and the face side of the frame. Less certain, but still worth trying, is to glue strips of newspaper to the underside of the mesh, relying on the contraction of the paper to pull things tight.

If, after everything has been tried, the mesh still feels slack, this is not quite the end; the screen may yet respond to one of the professional printer's emergency remedies. Mix up the printing colour rather thicker than usual, use a squeegee with a sharp, stiff blade, and print with maximum pressure. If the stencil floods every time when the squeegee is pulled in the normal direction, try pulling across the screen from side to side. There are four possible squeegee strokes, north, south, east and west, and all these strokes should be investigated so as to find which gives the best print. If flooding persists, no matter which stroke is used, cut two long strips of $\frac{1}{4}$ in. foam sheeting (foam rubber) about 1 in. wide, and fasten them to the underside of the mesh with masking tape or latex adhesive. They should go right across the screen from side to side, running parallel, and spaced apart at a distance slightly greater than the span of the squeegee blade. In this way the mesh is supported clear of the paper except at the moment when the squeegee blade is actually passing overhead. With a bit of luck this remedy should work like a tonic.

It is a rare thing for a stencil to fill the whole area of the mesh; there will almost always be a gap between the outside edge of the stencil and the inside edge of the screen frame, and this gap has to be closed with a suitable filler. The choice of filler depends on the job.

When printing with oil or cellulose colours, the quickest and easiest way to fill the gap is to use ordinary 2 in. wide gummed paper strip. Cut four pieces slightly longer than the four sides of the stencil. Wet them thoroughly by passing them through a basin of cold water, and lay them out on the bench to soak for a minute, gummed side up. Then lay them carefully on the mesh so that they overlap the edges of the stencil by $\frac{1}{2}$ in., and blot them gently with a pad of dry cloth. Continue in the same way adding more strips to the outside of the first set until the gap is closed. Make sure that each strip overlaps the previous one by about $\frac{3}{8}$ in. Finally, cover the strips with a couple of sheets of newspaper, and press for a few moments with a moderately cool iron. Some printers lay the gummed strip on the inside of the screen, others on the underside: it is a matter of personal preference. Generally speaking, it is better to leave the inside of the screen quite clear, so that the squeegee can have an uninterrupted run in contact with the mesh throughout its stroke. It is easier to get the strips to stick to the underside of the mesh if the screen can be supported upside down on a flat-topped block while the work is being done.

The gap can also be closed with a water-soluble filler such as fish glue (isenglass) or Autotype 752 blue screen filler. These fillers should be applied with a coating trough or scraper. Two or three coats may be needed.

When printing with a water-based colour, the gap must be closed with a waterproof filler such as shellac, screen lacquer, or polyurethane varnish. The gelatine/bichromate and PVA/bichromate coatings can also be used for this purpose. They should be applied in the usual way by coating trough or scraper, and hardened by exposure to the light. Two or three coats may be needed.

It is worth going to a lot of trouble at this stage to make sure that the screen really is watertight, because nothing is more exasperating than a screen that springs a leak half way through an edition. Particular attention should be paid to the line where the mesh meets the frame, and this line should always be covered with masking tape or gummed paper strip. Fold the strip in half lengthwise, and press it into the angle, so that one half lies flat on the mesh and the other half runs up the inside of the screen frame.

Hold the screen up to the light, and examine the stencil inch by inch. Any pinholes must be touched up with screen filler. Look along the underside of the mesh to see that knife-cut stencils are adhering properly. Look to see that nothing is obstructing the open parts of the stencil. If anything needs to be done, now is the time to do it.

Supposing a screen does start to leak half way through an edition, it may be possible to cover the hole with a patch of masking tape applied to the underside of the mesh. A scrap of typewriting paper smeared with a thin film of Copydex or Cow Gum (or, in the US, Elmer's Glue) will do the job just as well. A patch is a quick way of dealing with trouble in the margins, but if the trouble occurs in the stencil itself, the repair work must be done with a liquid filler.

Cover the printing bed with four or five thicknesses of old newspaper, and lower the screen into contact. Remove the printing colour by rubbing the inside of the mesh with a piece of cotton rag dipped in the appropriate solvent and squeezed partly dry: there is no need to swamp the screen. Change the rag and the newspaper as often as necessary, and continue until the mesh is both clean and dry. Do not on any account rub the underside of the screen, or the stencil will be damaged.

If oil or cellulose colour is being used, the repair work can be done with fish glue, gouache or tempera colour, or with one of the proprietary water-soluble screen fillers. If water-based printing colour is being used, the repair work can be done with shellac, rubber solution, or quick-drying varnish. A warm air blower will speed up the drying of the filler.

When printing is resumed after a pause for emergency repairs, or indeed after a pause for any other reason, the first thing to do is to run off a few test prints on waste material.

Everything possible must be done to give the squeegee a clear, straight run up the screen. Any irregularity in the bed, or in the stencil, or in the surface being printed, will cause the squeegee to shudder, and the result will be a bar or a series of parallel bars of deeper colour crossing the print from side to side. Register stops are thick enough to cause this trouble, and they should always be set at the extreme ends of the print paper, well clear of the picture space. The print paper must be large enough to allow for this. A reasonable working margin would be one inch on all four sides, and this can be trimmed off afterwards if necessary. But printing right up to the edge of the sheet is not a practical proposition.

As the squeegee objects to riding over any kind of irregularity, printing on thick board presents a special problem. The best solution is to build up on the bed a flat frame or mount fitting up against the edges of the board to be printed. The surface of this temporary frame should be level with the surface of the board to be printed, and the easiest way to achieve this is to make it from offcuts of the same material as the board itself. If there are no offcuts available, cardboard can be used instead, provided it is built up to the proper level. The frame should be not less than two inches wide at each end of the squeegee stroke, one inch wide along the two long sides. Take one of the boards to be printed and set it carefully on the printing bed so that it coincides with the image on the screen. Slide the offcut strips up against the edges of the board and fix them to the bed with a temporary adhesive. Adjust the hinge bar to the new raised level so that when the screen is lowered it will lie snug and flat. Fix a couple of scraps of offcut material to the printing bed immediately under the two front corners of the screen frame. The squeegee now has a smooth surface to run over. When it comes to printing, the boards are laid one after another in the space in the temporary frame. There is no need to set up any other kind of register guide.

At the beginning of its stroke the squeegee must be given a space of at least three inches to gather up the colour and get into its stride: it should have another three inches clear run at the end of the stroke after it has crossed the stencil. Like a runner, it should be going at full speed as it passes the finishing line. If the pressure is relaxed too soon, the print will flood. This means that the wells should be as broad and generous as the job will allow. Trying to print with a stencil that almost fills the screen is simply asking for trouble.

Textile printing is done by two printers facing each other across the long table and working together as a team. The screen is lowered into position, and each print is normally given two strokes with the squeegee, one out and one back. The assistant pulls the first stroke, and the senior printer then pulls the squeegee back to his side. Thus, each stroke is a pulled stroke. The squeegee is gripped as near the ends as possible, the arms are kept straight, the feet together, and the strain is taken in a natural and symmetrical manner by the whole body.

When printing an edition of individual sheets the squeegee is normally handled by one man. Where he should stand, and how he should hold the squeegee, is decided by a number of considerations: the size of the screen, the size of the stencil, the position of the hinges and, not least, the idiosyncrasy of the printer himself. There can be no absolute right and wrong in this matter. The best squeegee stroke is the one that gives consistently the best results in the shortest time, week in and week out, under ordinary workshop conditions.

In most commercial print works, the screens are large and hinged on one of the long sides. The printer stands at the middle of the other long side, and pulls the squeegee past him, from right to left. One pull should be sufficient: to give a second pull increases the consumption of colour, increases the time on the job, and introduces the risk of a blurred or double impression. At the end of the stroke the screen is raised, the print removed and the next sheet placed in the register stops. All this time the squeegee and pool of colour are waiting in the well at the left-hand end of the screen. The screen is now lowered again and, if the printer is ambidextrous, the next print is made by pulling the squeegee back across the mesh from left to right. This is the quickest way of working.

If the printer is not ambidextrous, the squeegee and pool of colour must be returned to their starting point at the right-hand end whilst the screen is held in the raised position. There are two ways to do this:

1 Lift the screen, take out the previous print, keep the screen raised. Now, using the

squeegee as a shovel, lift the pool of colour and carry it quickly through the air and drop it in the right hand well.

2 Lift the screen as before. Now, trailing the squeegee at a low angle, say about 30°, and using very soft pressure, sweep the colour back across the mesh from left to right. The effect of this stroke is to leave a considerable film of colour suspended in the mesh, ready to be pressed through when the next print is made. This method is sometimes called 'flood coating'. The beginner should try both methods, and compare the resulting prints.

The screen process uses a greater bulk of printing colour than any other printing process, and at any time in the course of a production run there may be anything up to a pint of colour in circulation in the screen. If the printer is not very careful, some of this colour will quickly find its way on to the handle of the squeegee, and from there it will not be long before it is all over the printer's clothes, and all over the prints. The handle of the squeegee *must* be kept clean. It may be possible to prop it up against the screen frame at the end of each stroke, but if there is the slightest risk that it might fall into the pool of colour, some kind of clip or hook or support must be provided. Every printer has his own ideas about this; some use a cupboard door catch, others an elastic band, others a couple of nails. Perhaps the most ingenious idea is the magnetic squeegee rest manufactured by Vista Display Signs Ltd of Basford, England.

At the moment when the squeegee has just completed its stroke, there is always a tendency for the newly made print to stick to the underside of the mesh. Getting the two to come apart cleanly is not quite as simple as beginners sometimes suppose.

When using a large screen to print a 'blotch' pattern on a length of textile fabric, the adhesion between the mesh and the newly made print may be so powerful that the screen will refuse to come up off the table with a straight lift. If this should happen, ease the frame up gently by one edge and hold it like that for a moment; the mesh will then separate itself naturally. It is a mistake to try brute force.

When printing on individual sheets with an ordinary screen hinged at the back, it is very easy to spoil a good print in the act of getting it off the mesh. As the screen is raised, the print may start to come up with it, and then fall off. If this should happen, the print will almost certainly suffer in one way or another. If the design consists of fine lines and dots, these will look as if they have been dragged or brushed. If the design consists of large flat areas, these may be defaced by mysterious bands and patches of thin, mottled colour, looking rather as if somebody had sat on the print.

There are two things to be done to avoid all this trouble. The first is to hold the sheet down on the bed so that it cannot be lifted by the screen. An amateur working at home with improvised equipment can coat his printing bed with one of the 'permanent' adhesives, such as Drystick Extra from Screen Process Supplies Ltd (trade name, UK. There are a number of 'permanent' adhesives available in the US). This substance is spread out as a thin even film and left for a couple of hours to dry. It dries with a permanently tacky surface which will hold any sheet pressed against it, without leaving a trace of itself on the back.

Trade printers work on a table with a suction bed, and any serious amateur who has ever worked on one of these tables will want to buy or make one for himself. A shallow airtight box is built on the underside of the bed. The surface of the bed is marked out with a $\frac{1}{2}$ in. square grid and drilled at every intersection with a $\frac{1}{16}$ in. bit. The holes are drilled right down into the cavity of the shallow box. A powerful electric pump extracts the air from the box and when a sheet of paper is laid on the surface of the bed it is held in place by the partial vacuum underneath.

The other thing that can be done to ensure a clean separation between mesh and wet print is to set the screen a fraction of an inch above the level of the bed. Take four small off-cuts of card or plywood, and tape them to the underside of the screen frame, one at each corner. On a small screen the offcuts should be about $\frac{1}{16}$ in. thick; on a large screen they might be as thick as $\frac{1}{4}$ in. A hinged screen can be raised at the back by packing up the adjustable hinge bar: the front can be raised by offcuts taped either to the underside of the frame itself, or to the place on the bed where the frame will come down. In this way the mesh is prevented from touching the surface of the printing bed except at the moment when the edge of the squeegee blade is actually passing overhead. As soon as the squeegee has passed the mesh springs clear again, with a characteristic sound which the old printers used to call the 'snap up'. To get the best results this technique should be used in conjunction with a vacuum printing table, or a table coated with a 'permanent' adhesive.

In the early days, a beginner may expect to spoil up to 10% of his prints, but with the passage of time and with constant practice the proportion should fall to somewhere around 1%. A percentage of spoils will turn up in every colour printed, and it follows therefore that the wastage in a five-colour job will be five times as great as the wastage in a job of one colour. When you are planning an edition allow plenty of spares: there is nothing worse than to end up with ninety-nine prints when a hundred had been promised.

As soon as printing has been finished for the day the screen and squeegee should be taken to be cleaned. The whole of this work should be done at the cleaning bench, and *not* on the printing table. Any worthwhile colour left in the screen or on the squeegee blade should be scraped up with an offcut of cardboard and returned to the can in which it was mixed. Mixed colour should never be poured back into the stock cans of new colour, but a special shelf should be kept apart for odds and ends of mixed colour.

The order of cleaning a screen is always the same: first remove the printing colour, then remove the stencil.

Water-based printing colours, and emulsion colours of the Polyprint type should be cleaned in the sink. Begin with a prolonged and vigorous rinsing inside and out with a jet of cold water. At this stage, hot water must not be used on the emulsion colours, or the binding medium may set solid. Continue with a thorough wash in warm water to which has been added a little detergent. Obstinate patches can be attacked by scrubbing with a pair of nail brushes held face to face, with the mesh in between. Finish with another cold water rinse, and then stand the screen up on edge to drain. A fan can be used to speed up the drying process, but a screen should never be stood against a fire or a radiator.

The programme for removing oil-based colours, varnishes and thin film inks should run like this:

1 Lay the screen on the flat, non-absorbent top of the cleaning bench.

2 Flood the mesh with white (mineral) spirit or, better still, a screen wash from one of the specialist suppliers. Leave for 10 minutes to allow the solvent time to do its work.

3 Remove as much of the dissolved colour as possible, first with a piece of cardboard, then with cleaning rag. Take a fresh piece of rag, soak it in the solvent, and go over the mesh once more.

4 While the solvent is still wet, flood the inside of the screen with a strong solution of detergent in hot water. Scrub with a nylon or bristle brush. When the detergent solution is mixed with the oil in this way it first forms an emulsion and then drags the oil molecules into solution. If there is too little detergent the lather disappears and oil blobs float about. Add more detergent and the blobs will be emulsified and dissolved.

5 Take the screen to the sink, and rinse with warm water until the mesh is perfectly clean.
6 Clean the top of the cleaning bench.

Detailed advice on the removal of stencils has already been given in the chapters dealing with stencils. When the stencil has been removed, hold the screen up to the light, and scan it with one eye closed. Any solid specks still remaining should be attacked with screen wash followed by detergent. Scrub with a nylon or bristle brush, and rinse with warm water. *Never* use a wire brush.

'There are many who say they have learned the art without having been with a master. Do not believe them, for I give you this very book as example: even studying it day and night, if you do not see some practice with some master, you will never be fit for anything, nor will you be able with a good face to stay among the masters.'
CENNINO CENNINI *Il Libro dell'Arte o Trattato della Pittura*

British Suppliers

ALGINATE INDUSTRIES LTD, Walter House, Bedford Street, Strand, London WC2 (Manutex)

ALGRAPHY LTD, Willowbrooke Grove, London SE15 (Litho crayon and liquid litho ink)

P. & J. ARNOLD LTD, Stavordale Road, London N5 (Photo-engraving glue)

ASHWORTH-LYME MARQUETRY, Old Corn Mill, Newtown, New Mills, via Stockport, Cheshire (Screen printing equipment, fabric printing tables, steamers)

BLACKWELL AND CO. LTD, Sugar House Lane, Stratford, London E15 (Printing colours)

A. G. W. BRITTON, Shenton Street, Old Kent Road, London SE15 (Printing colours)

CELLON LTD, Kingston-on-Thames, Surrey (Printing colours)

CHAPLIN & CO. (RUBBER) LTD, 276 Camberwell Road, London SE5 (Squeegee rubber)

COATES BROTHERS (INKS) LTD, Easton Street, Rosebery Avenue, London WC1 (Printing colours)

DANE & CO. LTD, 1–2 Sugar House Lane, Stratford, London E15 (Printing colours and other materials)

D.E.P. LTD, Frith Park, Walton-on-the-Hill, Tadworth, Surrey (Astrafoil)

C. DERRICK LTD, Polo House, Prince Street, Bristol 1 (Cleaning waste)

E.G.K. (TEXTILE MACHINERY & ACCESSORIES) LTD, 256 Park Lane, Macclesfield, Cheshire (Textile adhesives)

A. GALLENKAMP & CO. LTD, Technico House, Christopher Street, London EC2 (Water jet filter pump)

GEORGE HALL (SALES) LTD, Beauchamp Street, Shaw Heath, Stockport, Cheshire (Mesh materials and other screen process supplies)

SAMUEL JONES & CO. LTD, New Bridge Street, London EC4 (Gummed and coated papers)

JOHN T. KEEP & SONS LTD, 15 Theobald's Road, London WC1 (Printing colours, varnishes, thinners, signwriters' materials)

F. G. KETTLE, 23 New Oxford Street, London WC1 (Paper and card)

KODAK LTD, Graphic Arts Sales Dept, Kodak House, Kingsway, London WC2 (Kodalith Film and other photographic materials)

T. N. LAWRENCE & SON LTD, 2–4 Bleeding Heart Yard, Greville Street, Hatton Garden, London EC1 (Fine print papers, printing colours, sundries)

MACCLESFIELD ENGINEERING CO. LTD, Athey Street, Macclesfield, Cheshire (Textile printing equipment)

E. T. MARLER LTD, 191 Western Road, Merton Abbey, London SW19 (Printing colours, mesh materials, plane, sundries)

M. E. MCCREARY & CO., 815 Lisburn Road, Belfast BT9 7GX (Polyprint colours)

D. O. NICOLL LTD, 50 Britton Street, London EC1 (Chemicals, sundries, equipment)

PAPERCHASE, 313 Brompton Road, London SW3 (Every kind of paper)

PHILIPS ELECTRICAL LTD, Century House, Shaftesbury Avenue, London WC2 (Mercury vapour and Photoflood lamps)

PRONK, DAVIS & RUSBY LTD, 44 Penton Street, London N1 (Mesh materials, chemicals, equipment, sundries)

A. J. PURDY & CO. LTD, 248 Lea Bridge Road, London E10 (Mesh materials, adhesives, chemicals)

SCREEN PROCESS SUPPLIES LTD, 24 Parsons Green Lane, London SW6 (Everything for the screen process)

SELECTASINE SILK SCREENS LTD, 22 Bulstrode Street, London W1 (Printing colour, mesh materials, equipment, sundries),

SKILBECK BROTHERS LTD, Bagnall House, 55 & 57 Glengall Road, London SE15 (Helizarin printing colours, dyestuffs, thickenings)

VISTA DISPLAY SIGNS LTD, Springfield Works, Radford Road, Basford, Nottingham (Hinge assembly unit)

WINSOR AND NEWTON LTD, 51 Rathbone Place, London W1 (Printex printing colours)

American Suppliers

AMERICAN CRAYON COMPANY, 9 Rockefeller Plaza, New York, NY (Textile colors)

AMERICAN SCREEN PROCESS EQUIPMENT COMPANY, 1439 West Hubbard Street, Chicago 22, Ill. (Press equipment and supplies)

BECKER SIGN SUPPLY COMPANY, 319–321 N. Paca Street, Baltimore 1, Md. (General supplies)

BOURGES COLOR CORPORATION, 80 Fifth Avenue, New York, NY (Bourges color sheets and related supplies)

CELLO-TAK COMPANY, 431 West 20 Street, New York, NY (Transfer type and shading sheets)

CINCINNATI SCREEN PROCESS SUPPLIES, INC., 1111 Meta Drive, Cincinnati, 37, Ohio (Drying ovens and related products)

COATING PRODUCTS, INC., 275 Lincoln Blvd, Middlesex, NJ (Adhesive papers and related supplies)

CUDNER AND O'CONNER COMPANY, 4035 W. Kinzie Street, Chicago 24, Ill. (Lacquer and plastic inks)

B. DRAKENFELD & COMPANY, 45–47 Park Place, New York 7, NY (Screen fabrics, ceramic colors, decal papers)

DRY SCREEN PROCESS, INC., 801 Brighton Road, Pittsburgh, 33, Pa. (Screen-etched circuit supplies)

E. I. DU PONT DE NEMOURS & COMPANY, INC., 2410–17 Nemours Building, Washington 98, Del. (Photo films and related supplies)

EASTMAN KODAK COMPANY, Rochester 4, NY (Photo films and related supplies)

FILMOTYPE CORPORATION, 7500 McCormick Boulevard, Stokie, Ill. (Photo-lettering machines and related products)

GRAPHIC EQUIPMENT OF BOSTON, INC., 22 Simmons Street, Boston 20, Mass. (Presses and related equipment)

GRIFFIN MANUFACTURING COMPANY, 1658 Ridge Road, E. Webster, NY (Stencil knives and related instruments)

HOBART PAPER COMPANY, 111 W. Washington Street, Chicago 3, Ill. (Waterproof paper and related products)

INTERCHEMICAL PRINTING INK CORPORATION, 67 West 44 Street, New York, NY (Paints and related products)

KENRO GRAPHICS, INC., Cedar Knolls, NJ (Cameras and related products)

KLEENSTIK PRODUCTS COMPANY, 7300 W. Wilson Avenue, Chicago 31, Ill. (Self-adhesive products)

KRESSILK PRODUCTS, INC., 73 Murrary Street, New York, 7, NY (Screen fabrics)

LAWSON PRINTING MACHINE COMPANY, 4453 Olive Street, St Louis 8, Mo. (Printing equipment)

MCLOGAN'S SCREEN PROCESS SUPPLY HOUSE, 1324 S. Hope Street, Los Angeles, 15, Calif. (General supplies)

M. & M. RESEARCH ENGINEERING COMPANY, 13360 W. Silver Spring Road, Butler, Wisconsin (Presses and related equipment)

NORLAND PRODUCTS INC., P.O. Box 145, North Brunswick, NJ 08902 (Photoengraving glue)

NU-ARC COMPANY, INC., 4110 W. Grand Avenue, Chicago 51, Ill. (Photo equipment)

NU-FILM PRODUCTS COMPANY, INC., 56 W. 22 Street, New York 10, NY (General supplies and stencil film)

F. H. PAUL AND STEIN BROS., INC., 235 Fifth Avenue, New York 16, NY (Screen fabrics)

PHOTOX PHOTOGRAPHIC STENCIL FILM, 30 Irving Place, New York 3, NY (Photo stencils and supplies)

PRINTING AIDS CORPORATION, 9333 King Street, Franklin Park, Chicago, Ill. (Printing consultants and equipment)

PROTYPE GRAPHICS, 305 E. 45 Street, New York, NY (Photo-lettering equipment)

SERASCREEN CORPORATION, 147 W. 15 Street, New York 11, NY (General supplies and equipment)

T-W SCREEN PROCESS SUPPLY COMPANY, 9601 S. Stanford Avenue, Los Angeles, Calif.. (Decal paper and supplies)

ULANO PRODUCTS COMPANY, INC., 610 Dean Street, Brooklyn, NY (Stencil films and related supplies)

WILLMANN PAPER COMPANY, 308 W. Broadway, New York 12, NY (Paper and board)

WIRE CLOTH ENTERPRISES, INC., 3408 Penn Avenue, Pittsburgh 1, Pa. (Metal screen fabrics)

Bibliography

AUVIL, KENNETH W., *Serigraphy: Silk Screen Techniques for the Artist* Prentice-Hall, New Jersey, 1965

BAKER, F. A., *Silk Screen Practice* Blandford Press, London, 1934

BELONIS, ANTHONY, *Technical Problems of the Artist: Technique of the Silk Screen Process* Art Circular No. 6, USA Works Progress Administration, Washington, 1941 (typescript)

BIEGELEISEN, J. I., *The Complete Book of Silk Screen Printing Production* Dover Publications, New York, 1963

BIEGELEISEN, J. I., and COHN, M. A., *Silk Screen Techniques* Dover Publications, New York, 1958

BOLAM, F. (editor), *Paper Making* Technical Section of the British Paper & Board Makers' Association Inc, London, 1965

CARR, FRANCIS, *A Guide to Screen Process Printing* Studio Vista, London, 1961

COOK, J. G., *Handbook of Textile Fibres* Merrow, Watford, 1959

COUPE, R. R., *Science of Printing Technology* Cassell, London, 1966

DAVIDSON, E. A., *A Practical Manual of House Painting, Graining, Marbling and Sign Writing* Technical Press, London, 1947

DOERNER, MAX, translated, Dr Eugen Neuhaus, *The Materials of the Artist* Rupert Hart-Davis, London, 1949; Harcourt, Brace & World, New York, 1949

EDER, J. M., translated, Edward Epstean, *History of Photography* Columbia University Press, New York, 1945

ENTWISLE, E. A., *The Book of Wallpaper* Arthur Barker, London, 1954

GERNSHEIM, HELMUT and ALISON, *The History of Photography* Oxford University Press, London, 1955

HICKS, E., *Shellac* Macdonald, London, 1962: Chemical Publishing Co., New York, 1961

HIETT, HARRY L., edited, H. K. Middleton, *Silk Screen Process Production* Blandford Press, London, 1950, 1960

JOHNSTON, MEDA PARKER, and KAUFMAN, GLEN, *Design on Fabrics* Reinhold Publishing Co., New York, 1967

KENNEISON, W. C., and SPILMAN, A. J. B., *Dictionary of Printing, Papermaking and Bookbinding* George Newnes, London, 1963

KINSEY, ANTHONY, *Screen Printing*, Batsford, London, 1967; Watson-Guptill, New York, 1968

KNECHT, E., and FOTHERGILL, J. B., *The Principles and Practice of Textile Printing* Charles Griffin, London, 1912, 1924, 1936, 1952

KOSLOFF, ALBERT, *The Art and Craft of Screen Process Printing* The Bruce Publishing Co., New York, 1960

MAYER, RALPH, *The Artist's Handbook of Materials and Techniques* Faber & Faber, London, 1951, 1962; Viking Press, New, York, 1957

MIDDLETON, H. K., *Silk Screen Process: A Volume of Technical References* Blandford Press, London, 1949

RUSS, S., *Fabric Printing by Hand* Studio Vista, London, 1964; Watson-Guptill, New York, 1968

SOWERBY, A. L. M. (Editor), *Dictionary of Photography* Iliffe, London; Philosophical Library, New York, 18th edition, 1956

SPON, E. and F. N., *Workshop Receipts for Manufacturers and Scientific Amateurs* 4 vols, Spon, London, New York, 1909–1930

STEPHENSON, JESSIE BANE, *From Old Stencils to Silk Screening* Charles Scribner's Sons, New York, 1953

TATTON, W. H., and DRES, E. W., *Industrial Paint Application* George Newnes, London, 1964; Hart Publishing Co., New York, 1968

TAUSSIG, W., *Screen Printing* Clayton Aniline Co., Manchester, 1950

VERRY, H. R., *Document Copying and Reproduction Processes* Fountain Press, London, 1958

WIBORG, FRANK B., *Printing Ink* Harper & Brothers, New York, 1926

WITHERS, GERALD (Editor), *Screen Printing Point of Sale and Industrial Manual* Batiste Publications, London, 1967

WOLFE, HERBERT J., *Printing and Litho Inks* MacNair-Dorland Company, New York, 1957

Index